Marion Dean
Marion Pennington

Copyright © 2012

Marion Dean
www.trufflehuntersdogschool.com

ISBN: 978-0-9570323-0-9

Published by Marion Dean in conjunction with Writersworld,
this book is produced entirely in the UK, is available to order from most
book shops in the United Kingdom, and is also globally available via
UK-based Internet book retailers.

Art direction, Design and Photography by Nahim Afzal
www.nahimafzal.co.uk

Nahim Afzal design team: Nathan Appleyard & Bara Dudova

Illustration by Anna Nicolo & Bara Dudova
Food styling by Kirsty Thomas
Cover artwork checking by Jag Lall
Copy edited by Ian Large

www.writersworld.co.uk
Telephone: +44 (0)1993 812500
WRITERSWORLD
2 Bear Close Flats
Bear Close, Woodstock
Oxfordshire, OX20 1JX
United Kingdom

Discovering the Great British Truffle

Nature's best kept secret brought
to life for the contemporary kitchen

Marion Dean
&
Marion Pennington

I would like to thank the esteemed 'Team Truffle'
for their help in producing this book:

Our chef, Maz, for her recipes and high spirits.
Nahim for his most beautiful photography
and design. Kirsty for outstanding styling and
thorough recipe testing. Simon, for his advice
and vision. And, last but not least, my husband
Paul for stage design, hand modelling and tasting.

P.S. Mufti and Seven for snuffling the best truffles
in the land.

Marion Dean

————————————————

Foreword by Orlando Murrin

With the possible exception of manna, there has never been a food so steeped in glamour, mystery and charisma as the truffle. It is no surprise that something so rare and elusive should command an eye-watering price in French and Italian markets; but did you realize this magic foodstuff is indigenous to Britain – and very possibly growing in a wood near you?

No one is more passionate about truffles (some would say besotted) than the two Marions. In this fastidiously researched and lovingly written book, Marion Dean shares everything there is to be known about the British truffle: its history (which petered out in the 1950s, through lack of interest), a guide to the different varieties that grow in this country, their cultivation and growing conditions – and perhaps most compelling of all – how to find them. (Clue: enlist the help of a certain curly hound called Mufti.)

When it comes to truffle cookery, most existing recipes – if indeed you can find any at all among your cookbooks – are likely to be old-school French (think lobsters, *foie gras*, caviar...). Here at last is a collection of practical, modern, tested recipes that demonstrate the extraordinary potential of this remarkable – and subtle – ingredient. Whether you're looking for a quick fix with an egg or an elaborate showstopper for a dinner party, Marion Pennington has something delicious and inventive up her sleeve. And not a drop of crude, synthetic truffle oil in sight.

One of a thousand things I have learnt from reading this book is that the patron saint of truffles is St Anthony; he is also the patron saint of lost things. If it were not for the passion and generosity of our authors, this particular 'lost thing' – the British truffle – might well have remained in darkness for generations to come. Thank you for sharing it with British foodlovers.

Orlando Murrin is a food writer, editor and chef at Somerset's most exclusive gastro-hotel, Langford Fivehead, near Taunton.

An Invitation

Truffles in Britain?
Fantasy or fact?

Join us as we describe our journey of discovery into this nearly forgotten world of British truffles.

Your Hosts

Marion Dean

Marion Dean is the leading British authority on truffle hound training and runs a specialist school from her home in Somerset. Her truffling adventures take her all over the UK and have caught the attention of many European experts. She has a love of the countryside and a true delight for the surprises Mother Nature brings to the table. Her leading truffle hound is called Mufti, a slightly shaggy Lagotto Romagnolo.

Marion 'Maz' Pennington

Marion Pennington isn't one to be pigeonholed as a traditional chef. Her recipes are born from a natural understanding of flavour and a diverse European culinary upbringing. What's more, she'd tell you that Sev, her truffle hound, is the most valuable cooking apparatus she owns. Maz delights in experimenting with new flavours and combinations, daring to push the boundaries of traditional truffle recipes. She enjoys nothing more than sharing the delicious and original results with family and friends.

Contents

Prologue

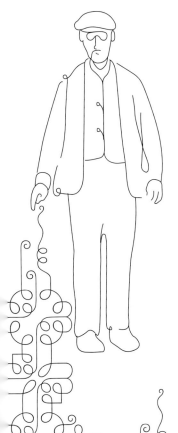

THE TRUFFLE HUNTERS OF WINTERSLOW

The title of the story caught my eye for two very good reasons. Firstly, it was about truffles and I was trying to find out about them. Secondly, I actually knew the village of Winterslow in Wiltshire because a friend of mine lives there. The link might have been a tenuous one but any link seemed better than none, so I decided to read on.

The tale mainly centred around the Collins family who had lived in the Winterslow area for generations. In particular was Eli Collins, who reputedly began hunting truffles from the age of nine. On one occasion Eli found an exceptional truffle weighing about two pounds (nearly a kilogram) and this was sent to Queen Victoria.

Knowledge of truffle hunting tended to be passed from father to son and although Eli had several children, only one son, Alfred, took up the profession. Alfred is described as using two rather strange looking Spanish poodles as truffle hounds and had a pannier on the front of his bicycle for carrying the dogs on longer journeys. His journeys really could be long ones too. He is said to have worked across eight counties. He finally retired in about 1935 seeing no future in truffle hunting and when he died in the 1950s, his secrets went with him to the grave. He is often described as the last professional truffle hunter in Britain.

I did not learn much about truffles themselves from this story but the location and the relatively recent age of the tale told me that this was all highly relevant information. I soaked it up, this was no mysterious truffle tale. It had names. It had places. It had dates. I rang my friend in Winterslow and she promised to see if she could find out any more details for me. She was as good as her word and a couple of days later a sheaf of papers arrived in the post. More names. More places. It was sad to think that Alfred had seen no future in truffle hunting because I saw the whole of my truffle future springing up from these pages. Where one story ended, another was just about to begin.

PART ONE: INTRODUCING THE GREAT BRITISH TRUFFLE

From Raspberries to Truffles

Like so many other people in this country I had never really come across truffles. I knew they were a delicacy, I knew they were expensive, and if I had to guess I would have said they came from France and Italy. That is not a lot to go on when thinking of a change of lifestyle but the reality was that my life had already been changed for me. Rheumatism had completely ended my lifelong love affair with horses and the battle back to some degree of fitness had taken several years. There was a rather large void just waiting to be filled. The story of the Truffle Hunters of Winterslow served to confirm my newly found feelings that planting a truffle orchard was a good idea. If I'm honest my mind was already made up. My heart had made a headlong jump into the truffle world and the rest of me was trying to catch it up. Let me explain.

Once an outdoor person, always an outdoor person. That made recovering from illness very frustrating. As soon as I was able, I made it outside to start fiddling about with plant pots, carrot seeds and the like. This was a new pastime and a little success went a long way. Once you have grown your own food there is no turning back and even if my carrots didn't look quite like the pictures on the packets they tasted wonderful. In a remarkably short space of time I was trying to grow just about everything I could think of. I had pots all over the place, fruit planted here, vegetables planted there, and even a few baskets hanging from above.

Gardening was not my total heart's desire but I did enjoy myself. Sadly it was not long before disaster struck and my raspberries started looking desperately poorly. This was devastating because I ate them in large quantities. One doesn't need to know a lot about gardening to recognise dead. If the raspberries were not dead yet, they soon would be.

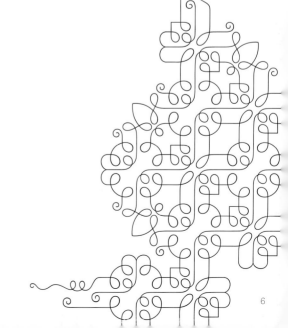

My husband Paul was the one to take action. He invited over a very keen gardener who had a most productive allotment. We were bound to get the best possible advice going. Now I don't know what my husband said behind my back, but something seemed to warn Len that he was dealing with someone in the hopeless-doesn't-know-a-thing group. I can't have been all that bad because he confirmed that my 'dead' diagnosis on the raspberries was correct. He also took the time to have a look at everything else I was doing, but I don't think he was very impressed. Out of the back of his car came an unusually large pile of gardening magazines and he left with the kind suggestion that I should read a few. It is a peculiar habit of mine that I often start reading magazines from the back. I think it's because I hold them in my left hand and fan through the pages until a picture catches my eye. This time I didn't have long to wait. Magazine one. At the back. There was an article about truffles. Not eating them, but growing them! Well, lights flashed, bells rung. Call it a eureka moment if you like. In fact call it anything you like, I was gripped. Perhaps I should write 'gripped' in capital letters to give you some sense of the impact this information had on me. GRIPPED. Here was my destiny, here was my new life. Instant decision. Growing truffles simply had to be more exciting than even carrots and raspberries put together. Now, I rarely do anything by halves and this occasion proved to be no exception.

I read and re-read the article. It got better each time. Why had I wasted all my life on horses? Here was something that would really be a good idea and was even supposed to give you a return, yes, and in large quantities, on your investment. No longer would the empty, horse-less, paddocks bring tears to my eyes. My mind saw them neatly planted up with rows and rows of soldier-like, truffle impregnated, oak trees. All I needed was a pile of money bags for the future large quantities of dosh.

There was a phone number. I dialled it. It was the first of many phone calls that the poor Dr. Thomas had to put up with. My empty fields were good, the operative word there being 'empty', but just about everything else was bad. Dr. Thomas broke the news very gently as I described the land – solid, badly drained clay with very large ancient oak trees on every perimeter. Of course there were measures that one could take to improve the land but it soon became abundantly obvious that all the improvements needed spelled out the horrible truth that my truffle orchard required a little more planning. If you think this in any way put me off, think again. I still knew I would have an orchard, somehow. My impetuosity is only matched by my stubbornness. 'No' was not on the agenda.

I won't call my next decision a compromise. It was the start of forward planning. I bought six, truffle impregnated, hazel bushes from Dr. Thomas. The reason was simple. I knew that having to improve the land would deprive me of at least one planting season and I could not bear the thought of delay. The hazels were to be grown on in pots to gain me more thinking time. I had to accept that planting them out later on might set them back a little, however I thought I would make an overall gain considering the time-line for truffle production is a very long one.

I told everyone I met I was going to have a truffle orchard. My friends were very supportive. They may well have considered that this little escapade sounded more strange than normal but they listened and had the grace to say they thought it was a good idea. You have already heard how I had learnt about the Truffle Hunters of Winterslow. Needless to say it was another friend who casually mentioned the following magical words to me.

'Truffle Hound.'

I don't think I need to tell you how I reacted to this (lights, bells, eureka etc.). For the second time I flew into action.

My Journey Begins

Dear sadly-departed Danny had been gone for a couple of years. He was a much loved, totally useless, soppy black Labrador, bred from a long line of non-gun dogs. His job was to be a family pet and he did that loyally for fourteen years. He only knew how to love; action never was high on the agenda. It often takes a while to replace a dog, and this was just the push I needed. I'm a great believer in saying some things are just meant to be. Lagottos, (the Italian hounds often used for truffle hunting) are not common in this country and one can sometimes be on a waiting list for a long time. There just happened to be a litter ready for homing and there just happened to be a puppy not yet spoken for. It all happened with indecent haste, but before I knew where I was, I was cuddling Mufti. My newly named, future little truffle hound superstar.

By now you may well have decided that I'm not fit to be let loose in the world, but I had not really been that reckless. In fact, every spare minute available had been spent doing truffle research on the internet. As subjects go, truffles must be the most difficult. Most of the important words are so long that your eyes would prefer to skip over them and they're just the ones in English. Latin features quite heavily too. No sooner do you read one fact and think you have got your brain around it, than you read something else contradicting the first. The situation was enough to drive anyone crackers. Eventually, many, many, many articles later, I was able to recognise authors who were just regurgitating something that they had read but did not understand either. It was a bit like tracing a family tree. For every tiny bit of information that was good, there were mountainous piles of the not-so-good.

Truffle cultivation, even here in Britain was not a new idea. People had been tackling the problem since the early nineteenth century. Success seemed to be very limited but fortunately for us it was noteworthy when achieved. Mr. Tillery of Welbeck recorded:

"In 1843 I commenced here an experiment of trying to induce Truffles to grow in a young Oak plantation near the lake, by getting all the parings and over-ripe ones from the kitchen, and planting them in it. The soil of this Oak plantation had originally come from the bed of the lake, and was full of the shells of small fresh-water molluscs, so that it was of a calcareous nature."

(Burbidge, F.W., *Cultivated plants: Their Propagation and Improvement.* W. Blackwood & Sons, 1877 [Reprint, Kessinger Publishing, 2008])

He could harvest two to three pounds (over one kilogram) of truffles when needed for his kitchen but noted how many small and unripe truffles were damaged by his spade because he did not have a trained dog to detect only the ripe ones. Mr. Tillery's success fuelled my ambition and I made a mental note about the damage he caused by harvesting with a spade instead of a dog.

I was able to find out far more about successful truffle cultivation in France. Even if techniques for growing truffles were relatively new, it was undeniable that there was a convincing new industry managing to evolve from an ancient country way of life. Somehow it came as no surprise to me that growing truffles was difficult. It seemed to fit the general picture that was building up in my mind. I suppose this was somehow in my favour. Let's face it, if it was easy to do, everyone would be doing it.

Now, some six years down the line, I have learnt a lot, and at least now I think I understand why so many problems exist. History, folklore and myth all play their part in creating a cloak of secrecy for the truffle to wear. Life would have been so much easier had Mother Nature decided to make truffles grow above the ground like my nice sensible raspberries.

What is a Truffle?

Let us spend a few moments looking at the truffle itself. For a start I should have used the plural for there are many, many different kinds of truffles. The field does narrow considerably if we restrict ourselves only to those types that are sought after for culinary use. Later in the book I will chart these main ones so that you can easily look up their names and characteristics. To start with I will talk in broad terms.

A truffle belongs to the fungus family. Think of it as an underground mushroom. It grows on the roots of certain kinds of trees e.g. oak, beech, hazel and silver birch. It forms a symbiotic relationship with the host tree. That means the tree and the truffle have a system of give and take, therefore both the tree and the truffle are important.

I have chosen the black Summer Truffle (*Tuber aestivum*) for this example because it's the truffle that Maz will be using in her recipes later on. The black outer casing is called the peridium. This is hard to the touch and is covered in pyramidal warts. Although this surface texture can vary, the overall feel is very rough. Indeed, the local Italian name for Summer Truffles is '*scorzone*' which literally translates as (tree) bark.

Slicing through the truffle reveals an intricate pattern of white veins and the coloured gleba. Gleba is the name given to the fleshy tissue which contains the truffle spores. When the black Summer Truffle is under-ripe the gleba is very pale, almost white. As the truffle matures and ripens, the gleba darkens to a rich brown colour and its aroma is released. Therefore the colour, flavour and aroma are all interrelated as the truffle develops. You may feel this last sentence is laboured or stating the obvious, but many people can become confused over it.

The truffle is affected by everything it is in contact with and everything else that surrounds it. The size the truffle reaches will depend on both the nutrients available from the tree (the truffle has no access to sunlight) and the nutrients available from the soil, plus the warmth and moisture from the weather. Truffles do not all start developing at the same time, therefore it is quite possible to have a small ripe truffle at the same time as a much larger, but not so ripe truffle. Both would be reflecting the conditions they grew in. The aroma from each truffle will tell you which is which. The shape of the truffle can vary hugely. Given a very light, friable soil, the truffle will come out more or less spherical. Factors such as stones in the soil, big strong roots that won't budge, or too many truffles growing too close for comfort can all affect their shape. Nobbles and funny bits are not a problem, don't worry about them.

Once the truffle is out of the ground it stops growing and has a very short shelf life. It must be handled with speed and knowledge, and cooked with sympathy and understanding.

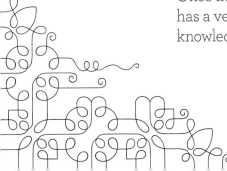

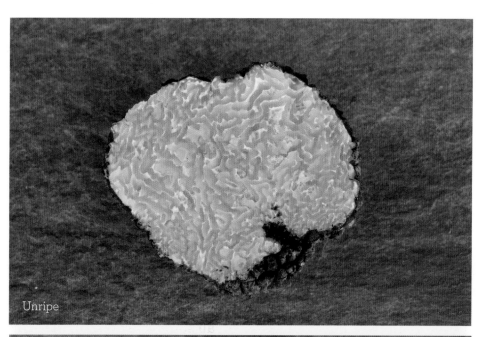

Unripe

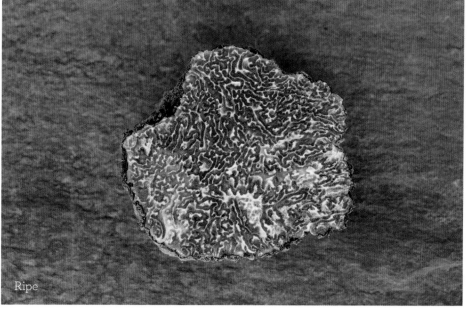

Ripe

BLACK MAGIC

As the truffle forms it is hidden from view. When the truffle matures, it is hidden from view. Dwell on these thoughts for just a moment or two. I am sure you will begin to appreciate some of the problems connected with truffles. Not only have they always been difficult to find, in ancient times it was also very difficult to explain their existence.

The learning of the day could not supply answers for a plant without a stem, without leaves or more importantly, without roots from which to grow. Reasoning therefore came from the unearthly – thunderbolts or even moonbeams struck the earth and brought truffles into being. By the Middle Ages a sinister association was made. Black and mysterious, truffles were not for God-fearing folk.

It really is quite remarkable how something as small as a truffle has caused so much consternation throughout time. Even now it continues its role of secrecy as its cultivation challenges many scientific brains of today. Truffles may be grown successfully in truffle orchards, but there is not a man on earth who has watched a truffle grow from start to finish – because they grow underground.

THE TRUFFLE AROMA

The truffle aroma is the key to all things truffly. The truffle is found when its aroma can be detected. At this point you may be smiling as I confirm the one fact that you were certain of, pigs were used for truffle hunting. But, do you know why pigs were used? Clever Mother Nature, she does come up with some good ones. The truffle aroma mimics the pheromones of pigs, therefore piggies of ancient times, happily feeding in woodland on acorns and beech masts would suddenly get hugely excited and snuffle up a truffle. Perhaps it was a piggy that first alerted man to the joys of eating truffles, who knows?

Of course piggies still are madly attracted to truffles, but the problem for man is that pigs like to live by the rule of 'finders, keepers' and eat what they consider to be rightfully theirs. Man lost too many truffles to pigs, and apparently more than a few fingers too (pigs have very sharp teeth and strong jaws) therefore a new answer was sought... truffle hounds! They are much easier to train than pigs and in most cases are happy to exchange a truffle for a reward. No, I have never used a pig for finding truffles, and yes, I am happy to report that I still have the correct number of fingers on each hand.

So far I have mentioned the truffle aroma a couple of times. The first time was to do with assessing the ripeness of a truffle and this time was to do with detection, or should I say, attraction. What may surprise you is another attribute it appears to have, the truffle aroma is well known for being very difficult to describe. Of course the different truffles each have different aromas, but even so, I think a room full of twenty people could give as many as twenty differing thoughts when trying to describe the aroma of a truffle. Not every description would be complimentary either! Muskiness is often mooted (hence the aphrodisiac association), and other body parts can also be mentioned, but I don't find feet particularly strong selling points. Hmmmm, perhaps the British are definitely more suited to the gentle hazelnutty overtones of our black Summer Truffle aroma!

At this point I could almost offer up a challenge. I don't think it's possible to hand any truffle connoisseur a truffle without their first reaction being to hold it to their nose and take a long deep inhalation. Many is the time I have been delighted by the response of very well known chefs when handing them an innocent little black Summer Truffle. Of course they immediately recognise the truffle as such, and then they take the 'compulsory' sniff test. At this point I can hardly keep my face straight as I watch their interest turn to curiosity and then to amazement. There's nothing quite like a good British black Summer Truffle for surprising even the best of chefs. I simply love it when I have the opportunity to answer the question, "Where did this come from?" And I can smile and say, "Just down the road..."

The Black Summer Truffle

Let us see if we can work out what happened to our native truffle supply and why to all intents and purposes truffles seemed to disappear almost completely from our culture.

We know that Alfred Collins, one of the Truffle Hunters of Winterslow, retired in the 30s. His work was well documented but of course he would not be the only one with a working knowledge of truffle hunting. I would imagine each good truffle producing area or large estate had its own followers. That word 'secrecy' appears time and time again! If knowledge is not freely available, when the holder goes, so too does that source of learning. What did happen to many holders of truffle knowledge, were the World Wars. The sudden, huge loss of life across all levels of society literally changed the world. Thereafter add to this the rapid development of technology, cars, washing machines, televisions and nearly everything else you can think of in our modern homes and you will see our lives centred on speed, cleanliness and convenience.

Of course the advent of much of this 'progress' had an adverse effect on the truffle. The black Summer Truffle is a woodland species. We built roads. We built houses. We built most things. Throughout this process a great deal of our native broadleaf woodland was lost forever. We did not even walk through the woods that were left; we drove past them in our cars. The truffle, to all but a tiny few, was comprehensively forgotten.

Admittedly, the black Summer Truffle in Britain had never had the popularity or the industry connected to it as, say, the truffles of France or Italy. Therefore when the knowledge was lost, there were not many to mourn its passing. Fortunately, although the truffle habitat suffered, the truffle itself survived. I am happy to report that over the years I have found truffles alive and well in many different parts of the country. There is nothing more wonderful than searching in an entirely new area and coming up trumps, or at least truffles.

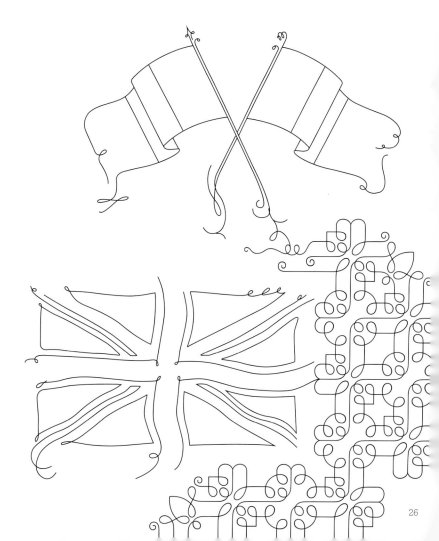

HERE AND NOW IN BRITAIN

The black Summer Truffle (*Tuber aestivum*), just mentioned,
is the most commonly found truffle in Britain. Names can be
a nightmare with truffles. We obviously name them in English
and then when needing to be technical or specific, we use
Latin for the genus and species. That ought to be enough for
anyone but truffles grow worldwide and so in many cases
local or descriptive names come into play too. It is possible to
end up with four or more different names for the same thing.
Other kinds of truffles grow in Britain too, but in my personal
experience, they are few and far between compared with the
black Summer Truffle. I have found some black Winter Truffles
(*Tuber brumale*), but I really don't like the smell of these ones.
In a commercial situation they tend to be processed. This
removes some of the unpleasant aroma, but they're still not
on my to-be-desired list. Please don't confuse these with THE
Black Winter Truffle, (*Tuber melanosporum*), aka the Périgord
Truffle of France. They are both black and they both ripen
over the winter months but there the resemblance ends. The
Périgord Truffle is one of the most sought after for culinary
use. At this time of writing, I do not know of any 'wild' Périgord
Truffle finds in this country that have been verified. However,
I do know of truffle orchards where these are hopefully
growing and won't that be a headline we can all rejoice in
when harvesting begins!

Still more rarely you might find mention of other truffle kinds such as the Smooth Black Truffle (*Tuber macrosporum*) and even Bianchetto (*Tuber borchii*) but I haven't been lucky enough – or in the right place – to find any of these. If you are now waiting for me to mention the ultimate White Truffle (*Tuber magnatum*), aka the Piedmont Truffle of Italy, I can only do so with sadness, it is not indigenous to these shores.

Tuber macrosporum

I have been mentioning truffles which grow here. None of 'our' truffles are restricted to these shores, indeed they grow widespread through the whole of Europe and beyond. Only a tiny, tiny minority of the truffles for sale in this country will have originated here. Talk truffles and you talk global.

Even if I have only named a few truffles you should now realise that it could be possible to buy the wrong kind or even eat the wrong kind if you were not careful about what you were doing. This may be an appropriate place to remind everyone to have expert advice when identifying any truffle or supposed truffle found growing naturally.

Tuber borchii

The Truffle Year

Which is the best truffle of all? If you ask
a Frenchman, the answer will be the Périgord
black truffle of France. If you ask an Italian,
the answer will be the Piedmont white truffle
of Italy. If you ask me, I will say a fresh one.
I think the 'best truffle' dispute will last as
long as man breathes, but I am sure everyone
will agree with me that the best way to eat any
truffle is as fresh as possible.

Join me on a journey through the British
Summer Truffle Year; that way you won't miss
a moment of fresh truffle opportunity, and
your only dilemma will be in choosing which
recipe to try first.

SPRING

March, April, May. I always enjoy the first true spring sunshine.
That is, not the weak watery, winter variety, more the warming
encouraging type, full of promises for the coming season.
I respond with some frantic work on the veg patch but I cannot
do the same for truffles. Unlike veg there is nothing I can do
to hasten the truffle season. Cloches and polytunnels are of no
use, and truffles don't come in seed packets. The time without
them must simply be endured.

At least in this respect we are very well off in this country,
the time without truffles can be very short, or put the other
way, the time *with* truffles can be generously long.

I often joke about finding disobedient truffles, that is, those
ones which obviously have not read the rulebook and do things
when we are not expecting it. Of course what I am really
saying is that either side of the summer truffles that should
ripen in summer are those early birds which I have found as
early as May and June, and more interestingly for me, the
late ones, which in this country can be very late indeed.

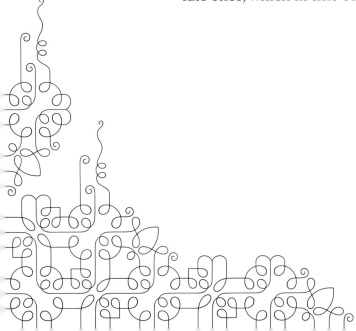

Dry weather can take a very severe toll on truffles. At this time of writing in 2012 the early truffles were few and far between. I am certain that this was due to the compound effect of a couple of low rainfall years, followed by an exceptionally dry winter. As anxious as I was to get underway with the new season, truffle progress was painfully slow. I can almost hear your outrage recalling the extreme downpours and floods widespread across Britain that spring – this rain was too late for my 'earlies' but we hoped it would help things along for the more traditional later harvest.

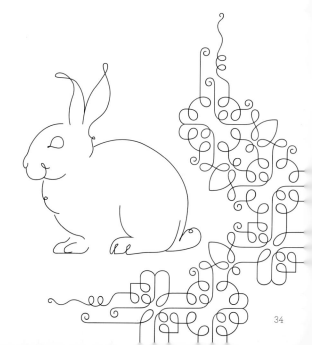

SUMMER

June, July and August. This season sees the start of prime time for British black Summer Truffles. Our truffles need a generous amount of rainfall to swell and mature – luckily that's something the British summer tends to provide in abundance. This, coupled with a pleasant ambient temperature, provides the perfect climate for some wonderful truffles.

I must admit that I am often drawn into campaign mode in the summer. Lots of people think Summer Truffles are pale ghostly things. Certainly on mainland Europe they are often harvested and eaten this way. To my mind this is a crime against truffles! Truffles presented in this way are yet to ripen and develop their full colour, flavour and aroma. My firm opinion is that if these truffles were left in the ground just a little while longer, they would taste oh so much better!

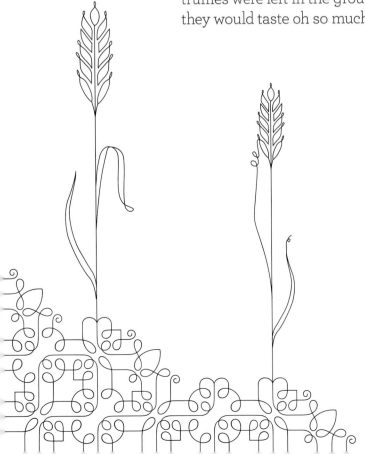

I must admit that I take absolute delight in unearthing a really good quality ripe black Summer Truffle. Every time it will impress those who are familiar with buying and preparing imported ones. Once introduced to the connoisseur, our home grown truffles are never forgotten. Oh, British Truffle, I am so proud of you.

The summer months are a good time for truffle virgins. You can try truffles at their most reasonable price. A little truffle goes a long way so you really do not need to break the bank to buy one. Heady reports of top international restaurants charging for each truffle shaving as it hits your plate actually helps to make you feel good as your own modest truffle provides dozens of shavings to pile up or spread as you wish. Should you have some to hand, I suggest you flick ahead to Maz's recipe section where she happily explains how to layer flavours and get the very most out of your truffle.

AUTUMN

September, October and November. Our 'season of mists and mellow fruitfulness'. Even if John Keats wrote those words before me, I am happy to second them. Autumn is my favourite season of the year and it makes me doubly happy that truffles can often be produced in very large quantities. The nights begin to draw in and the ambient temperature begins to lower, but by now the majority of British black Summer Truffles are coming into their own and ripening happily continues. Hand on heart I can say that some of the best black Summer Truffles I have found have ripened in the autumn.

At the beginning of autumn my task of finding truffles is an absolute joy. Once I have found the right kinds of trees growing in the right kind of soil (this is typically beech, oak, silver birch and hazelnut on chalk or limestone), I can start looking for other little truffle clues. We are not alone when it comes to the enjoyment of truffles! Small, saucer-shaped depressions show the nimble work of the rabbits and squirrels, whilst heavy excavations left by badgers and boar tell me I'm getting warm. One has to hope that there are plenty of our hidden truffle treasures to go round; after all, the wild animals are living on the job.

As autumn rolls on, these signs are harder to spot. Summer Truffles don't always create what's called a *brûlée*. No, we're not in the recipe section yet, but the word is the same as in *'crème brûlée'* – the pudding with the burnt sugar topping. In the truffle world it refers to what appears to be a patch of 'burnt earth', just under the tree without other plants growing in it. This is a prime indicator that truffles are below the soil. However, as the night frosts nip the air, the leaves begin to fall. The accumulating leaf litter is enough to make my job more difficult, covering animal diggings or a potential *brûlée*. Fortunately, the truffle harvesting happily continues – a dog's nose is not at all hampered by the thickest blanket of leaves and the truffles might even enjoy the extra protection from the weather. What I know for sure is that they keep on growing and their quality is excellent.

WINTER

Most things in life shut down over winter, but this isn't
always true for our truffles. And don't let names deceive you.
We started talking about the black Summer Truffle, and we
still are... Despite colder conditions, more frequent frosts,
and in recent years, deep snow, these truffles can be found
in December, January, and, on rare occasions, February.

On the other hand, actually locating them is not so easy.
For a start we're talking about much, much lower quantities
than in summer and autumn. Then there's the heavy leaf
litter and snow. Whilst making truffle discovery much
harder indeed, my hypothesis is that leaf and snow cover
can sometimes help insulate the truffles, allowing these
true stalwarts to keep on coming.

Unfortunately, not many others have had the opportunity to indulge in these discoveries. Nearly all of my extra, extra, extra late black Summer Truffles went straight to Maz's kitchen for culinary exploration – only home-sourced truffles were eaten during the writing of this book!

Perhaps I should call winter a quiet time, but don't let this deceive you. My personal opinion is that these months are absolutely vital for the coming season's truffles. While the leaves are on the ground and the tree canopy is open to the skies, the oh so valuable winter rainfall has direct access to the woodland floor. Now is the time when any over dryness of the soil from previous months can be corrected.

As winter draws to a close, we really can say goodbye to our Summer Truffle season. But only for a few a months. Before we know it, we're into spring and searching for our first truffly treats.

Let the Hunt Begin

Everything was beautifully prepared. My brother and I had worked as a team on this one. We sat quietly, motionless, behind some bushes, waiting. We could hear Ben approaching; he seemed to take forever as he studied the curious sugar lump trail. His tummy always won over any misgivings he might have been feeling as each step he took brought him nearer to us. At the right moment I was meant to pounce with a head collar, Lionel was anchorman (literally) and Ben was just a plain naughty pony.

Rarely did our pony entrapment techniques work. Ben ate all the sugar then hurtled away beyond our reach. Naughty ponies remain light years ahead of anything regular children can offer up. Parents called it character building, I remember it more as cruelty – to children, not the pony!

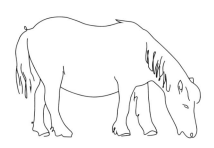

Four long years of owning this horrendous monster pony actually did do a lot for me. My sense of timing was lightning quick and I learnt to watch animals. Long before Monty Roberts showed us all the importance of body language with horses, I already knew that some times were right and some times were wrong, some ways were good and some ways were bad. To decide which was which you had to watch and listen. Attempt anything at the wrong time or place and you would inevitably be doomed to failure. I concede that between the ages of eight and twelve years old I singularly did not appreciate the lessons that Ben was teaching me but in reality he helped to pave the way for my future work with both horses and dogs.

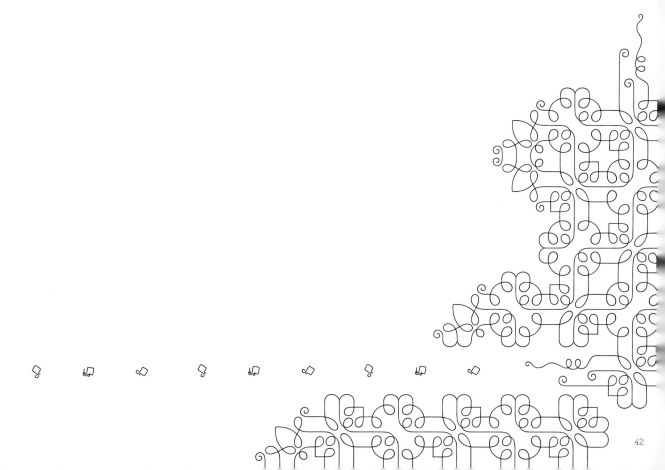

I think all of life is basically a series of problem solving. If you are good at something, the problems don't seem to be very big at all; if you are struggling, the problems seem to grow out of all proportion. Understanding problems is half the battle. When I was working with horses I always enjoyed a close sense of communication with them. Even if horses can't use words to tell you when something is wrong, they openly display fear, nervousness or ill health. The worst thing you can do is ignore them. You must look into the problem and either solve it yourself or ask someone else for help.

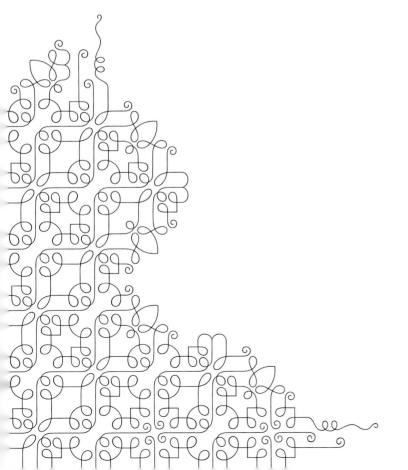

I had never had a 'working' relationship with a dog. Our family dogs had always been pets. As much as I always loved them, there were not many challenges involved. Now life had suddenly taken a most unusual turn and I found myself wanting to train my own truffle hound. This was totally new and totally different and needed a whole new specific training regime. I knew what I wanted to achieve, all I had to do was work out how I was going to do it.

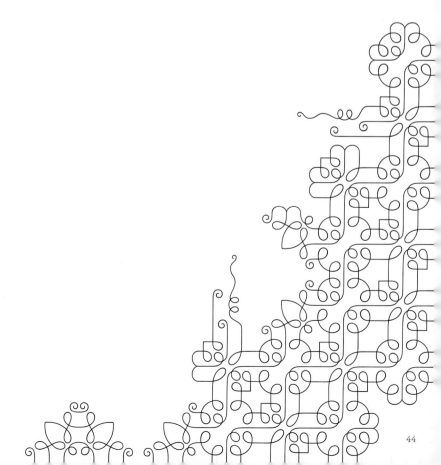

A Truffle Hound in the Making

Mufti was not the easiest puppy in the world; in fact she was quite a feisty little madam. It was probably a good thing that the list of things I wanted to teach her was a long one. I dread to think what a bored Lagotto could have been like. We were very fortunate to be close enough to the excellent Winchester City Dog Club to make our weekly journey for socialisation skills and the Good Citizens Award Scheme for dogs. Mufti loved it so much she actually gave me a really hard time during class as she vied for attention and wanted to be the centre of any fun going.

If reading magazines backwards is a bad habit of mine, so too is chewing pencils. It may not be recognised in many medical circles that this condition is in fact hereditary but it is. My son's school even rang me up about the number of pencils he ate during the course of a day. I failed miserably as a mother when I found this fact amusing.

I chewed my way through many a pencil as I prepared my dog training plan. I thought of Mufti's general skills as a dog and her more specific skills with scent. One doesn't train a dog how to find things with their nose – they know already. Throw a bone into your garden and any dog will find it pretty quickly. What I needed was for Mufti to tell me when she could smell a truffle. Words were not at her disposal – she could not shout, "Over here!" She had to give me a sign. In other words we had to develop a form of communication that we could both understand.

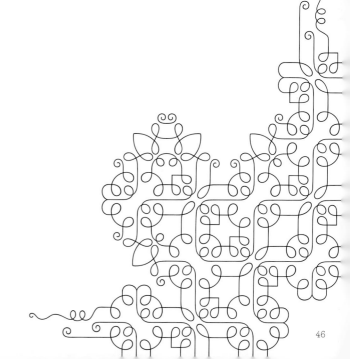

Once I had established the basics in my mind the rest of the training rather fell into place. I had to factor in all the niceties that I wanted to be present – such as a 'well-mannered dog quietly waiting beside the truffle it had just found', and I had to factor out any unwanted behaviour – such as 'dog eating truffle' à la piggy mode.

I must admit that Mufti took to all the training with indecent ease. By the age of five months she had mastered everything to perfection, the only concession I had to grant was that she considered it vital that everything must be completed at high speed. With one dog trained, it seemed like a logical decision to train others, and there lay the inspiration for Truffle Hunters Dog School. News of the Dog School brought more than a little media attention. While I suffered the normal 'tummy butterflies' through my very competitive desire to do well, Mufti charmed journalists, radio presenters and photographers as though it was all part of her job. I'm really glad I chose a puppy with a built-in flexible remit. The top and bottom of it all is the fact that she's not a truffle hound, she's a food hound – one piece of cheese and she will sell her soul! To this day I never take Mufti to meet a journalist without a healthy supply of cheddar in my coat pocket.

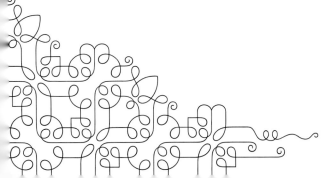

Those early truffle training days were wonderful in so very many ways, but to all intents and purposes I was working 'blind'. I was training dogs by using truffle oil for the scent. This method is absolutely valid, as nearly all truffle oil is chemically produced ensuring the smell is consistent with natural ripe truffle. But, what we had not yet done was to find a real live truffle. In our defence we had started before that season's truffles were ripe but it was a cause of great consternation that I could tell everyone what trees to look for, I could tell everyone what kind of soil conditions were best, I could tell everyone HOW a truffle grew, but neither Mufti nor I could tell you WHERE a truffle grew.

Picking up the Scent

I would not exactly describe myself as a hoarder but I did turn into an avid collector of truffle trivia. It did not matter whether the information was old or new; I decided everything had a value and perhaps one day it would eventually all fit together like a jigsaw. Just as I was able to relate to the story about the Truffle Hunters of Winterslow, the natural history writings of Gilbert White (1720–1793) also made quite an impact on me. A little more time had elapsed than with Alfred Collins' story here, but again the information was local to me. Gilbert White lived in the village of Selborne in Hampshire, a mere thirty minutes drive from my house. There are quite a few references to truffles in his work, mentioning truffles in both Selborne and Fyfield, near Andover where his brother was rector.

Even though I knew it was too early in the year to find any truffles, I often drove out to these villages to familiarise myself with their areas. I tried to find footpaths that would let me walk through some truffle-promising countryside. It not only had to have the right kind of soil but it also needed to have the right kinds of trees. Of course Mufti was always with me. Of course I always asked her to have a quick look for some truffles. Each time I would watch her intently just waiting to see if she plopped down in the indication style I taught her. There were many, many times when she didn't even slow down from a gallop let alone show any interest in, well, anything. She was an express truffle hound, but still without any truffles.

I found talking to people about truffles could be a double-edged weapon. 'Mushroomy' people listened avidly and shared with me the potential joy of finding my first truffle. I would often be told tales about how long it took them to find this or that. I was grateful for their empathy even though my only passion for mushrooms involves eating them. For such a forgotten skill I also met a huge number of 'truffle experts' who all delighted in telling me that there weren't any truffles in Britain. Instead of being sad about breaking this bad news to me, they actually found it hilariously funny. In this situation there isn't actually much one can say. It was a time frame fraught with expectation.

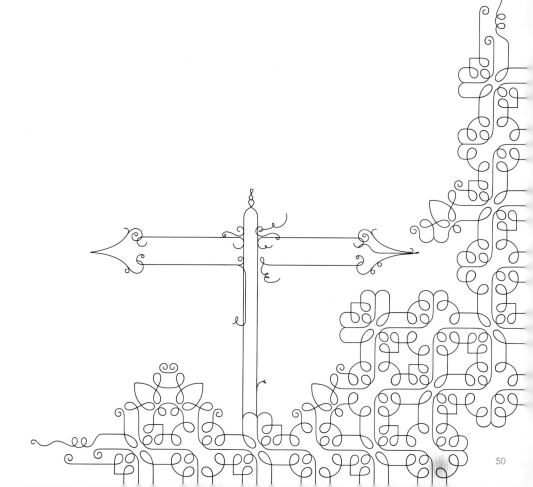

THERE BE TRUFFLES IN KENT

Very, very rarely did spoken truffle information seem any
more than folklore but there were a couple of snippets that
I mentally catalogued very carefully. One did in fact turn out
to be a very important part of my jigsaw. The tale was second
hand but not to be doubted. It related to the hurricane in 1987
– the one made famous by Michael Fish in his spectacularly
inaccurate hurricane-denial weather forecast! In one particular
Kentish woodland (note the truffle secrecy here) many beech
trees had been blown over and it was possible to gather truffles
off the exposed tree roots, so I was told. It was a ridiculously
long way to go on just a hunch, but local truffles seemed
stubbornly elusive. I decided a visit would be worth while and
chose a footpath that skirted the area I had been told about.
My thinking was that it was more off the beaten track and less
likely to be trodden by a million pairs of walking boots.

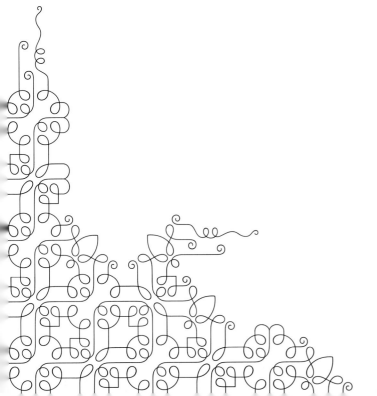

Mufti was her usual mile-a-minute self for quite some way until she slowed down and looked at me. She trotted on a couple of steps and then went back to where she had been. She looked at me again. This was different, she was moving slowly! She hoovered her nose in one direction then came back and hoovered the other way. She lingered. An imaginary question mark hung in the air above her head. Then... she went down in a perfect indication. My husband Paul and I were only a couple of yards away and it didn't take us long to cover the gap. The ground was only a little muddy as we probed and struggled with Mufti for the best truffle position. There it was, barely half an inch down, a moderately small, rather ugly, sorry, beautiful, life-changing truffle. Mufti went beside herself. So did Paul and I. We squeaked with delight and praised Mufti till she was dizzy. I'm glad there was no-one there to see us, but not because of anything to do with the secrecy – they would have taken us away to the funny farm, no questions asked.

Now Mufti fully understood her part of the partnership. She obviously had thought that all the training was just some kind of good fun game carrying the opportunity for lots of treats. Finding the truffle in the wood told her that this was for real and in that instant, she came of age.

Our journey home was one to remember. Mufti normally travels in the back of the car, but this time she wore her harness and sat on my knee in the front – Paul was driving. There was no doubt whatsoever that Mufti realised the enormity of what she had just achieved. She sat with her chest puffed out and every time we overtook another car she looked at the occupants as if to say, "I'm a truffle hound you know!" All that was missing was a regal wave.

No-one ever ate that first truffle of Mufti's. It was shown to all and sundry whether they liked it or not. By the time it had done the rounds for a couple of weeks, it wasn't a pretty sight. I don't think truffles will ever win any prizes for beauty and I did consider this one would by now be carrying every germ known to mankind. There are just times in life when one must face up to facts. What I had to do was obvious. In ceremonious mode I set off, complete with truffle and trowel, and made my own little burial site – carefully placing my now chopped up truffle in the soil surrounding the most ordinary-looking hazelnut bush I could find, location top secret. I'll go back with Mufti in a few years' time and see if any new truffles have grown from the spores in the original. The chances are remote in the extreme, but I would love it if history were to repeat itself.

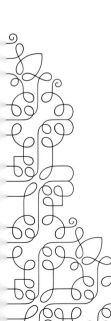

The Black Gold Rush

Back in Hampshire, things were progressing nicely with the Dog School. Perhaps St. Anthony, the Patron Saint of Truffles, was smiling down on me. From having no experience in the media spotlight I suddenly found that newspapers, magazines and television all enjoyed talking truffle. I must have been naïve not to see it coming. Several of my dog training days came complete with journalist or BBC camera crew. I don't actually feel any different about myself but my admiration for my dog has grown from every 'media' occasion. She never let me down. Can anyone please explain how a dog trained to find truffles also knows exactly when to say 'woof' into a Radio Solent microphone?

One day I remember fondly was when Maggie Philbin came to visit from Radio Berkshire. The morning turned out to be foggy which doesn't have the slightest effect on truffles, but it does affect one's ability to safely erect a portable radio mast. Fortunately we were able to reassure her that our power cables were underground so a relocation was not necessary. A brief thinning of the fog allowed a visual check and up went the mast. Seconds later, in a totally seamless fashion, Maggie was giving the morning's weather report, "...swirling fog, dense in places, otherwise patchy." I was filled with admiration for her total unflappability. Weather report over, she just continued talking to us where she had left off before. What a professional! We talked truffles, we ate bacon croissants, Maggie kept turning away to give another weather report, we ate more bacon croissants, and talked more truffles. It was sad the morning ever had to end; I rated it as the best.

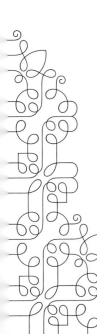

In those early days I was trying to do so many different things at once. Yes, I had established that I could train truffle dogs, but as soon as I had a little knowledge about truffles, I realised how much more there was to learn about them. Travelling abroad was almost a 'must'. Both France and Italy were the obvious destinations and I was soon to put the experience I gained there into good use in this country.

THE TRUFFLE CHAMPIONSHIPS

Knowing me I suppose it just had to happen. A Championship Dog Show? No, Truffle Hunting Championships? Yes, here in Britain and give me one good reason why not! I had been to the Truffle Championships for Lagottos in Italy, spending one exceedingly cold Sunday morning up an Italian mountainside and I had seen videos of an event in France. They used completely differing methods for testing and judging, so I decided I could devise my own contest that would ease people in gently to the concept that truffle hunting could be competitive. I was absolutely thrilled with the backup that I was given, both by the generous sponsorship from James Wellbeloved and the amazing participation from Forbury's Restaurant and Wine Bar in Reading who did cooking demos on field and served truffle tasters throughout the day. It sounds blasé to say that of course the TV cameras were there, my poor competitors had to be so brave! Fortunately the two people I had asked to do the judging for me, Anne Dicker and Andrew Wood, rose to the (unknown) challenge with both skill and grace. I think everyone went home happy; there were certainly plenty of smiling faces and perhaps that event was actually a marker to say that British truffles were back on the map.

One of those very brave competitors was actually 13 year old Sophie Bennet who was helping CBBC make a children's programme on truffles. One might think that being on television is hugely glamorous, actually it's hugely exhausting. Sophie won my lifelong admiration with how she coped with the situation, her mother and I both nearly buckled at the knees. To say that the programme was a success is an understatement and it threw up one of my favourite tales. It was seen by a school child, who obviously listened and learned. A short while after, in the school play area, she really, truly, unbelievably found a truffle and showed it to her teacher. Can you imagine the scenario? "Please, Miss, I've found a truffle." I sympathise with the teacher who was uncertain about identifying truffles but she fortunately acted correctly by passing the truffle to another member of staff who undertook the I. D. task. Where does one go for help? The nearest gastro pub of course! Her choice of hostelry was excellent, not only did the chef genuinely know about truffles, but also having some lunchtime refreshment was a previous customer from the Dog School who had just trained his Labrador puppy. He immediately recognised the truffle as good and urged the school to ring me up. This they did and the happy outcome of the story is that I harvest the truffles and the school receives regular cheques, which go towards the purchase of new equipment. What a result!

One of my aims in this book is to bring truffles into reality for my readers. I really hope that by now even my greatest detractors are grudgingly admitting that truffles are indigenous in this country and that it is perfectly possible to go out and find them. My preferred method of persuasion is to illustrate my point by a series of anecdotes and you might also realise just how much fun I've have in the meantime. This is one of my favourites.

No doubt I have many shortcomings in life, but one in particular often causes me no end of grief and that is the fact that I have no sense of direction. I really mean none. You would think if I can train a dog to find truffles I really ought to be able to train a dog to find my car but somehow it doesn't work like that. All my friends know that once I depart from home I really need the equivalent of a minder. No matter how hard they try I still manage to confound them. I regularly go out truffle hunting with Nicky Baxter. She was one of my very first customers and her Labrador, Dolly, developed into one of the best truffle hounds you could wish for. Many are the times that Nicky has suffered getting lost because of me, especially if she is driving and I am map reading. Never mind. On this particular morning she thought of an absolutely foolproof place for us to meet. A huge pub (yes they do crop up regularly in truffle stories) beside a major 'A' road would be impossible for me to miss. Yes, I missed it and drove on a further couple of miles to the next town before realising my mistake. As I was turning the car around for a second attempt at finding the pub, Nicky rang me up to say she was already waiting there.

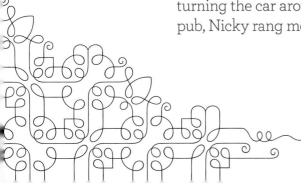

She assured me I was only a couple of minutes away and she would stand on the grass verge and wave as I approached. I approached. Nicky stood on the grass verge but she wasn't waving. In fact for a split second I wondered what was wrong. As I turned the car into the car park she raised one hand just a little. I immediately guessed what was in it! In the space of time it had taken me to drive down the road, Dolly had found a truffle under a beech tree. I'm often asked if a trained dog will tell you about a truffle find even if it is not under a 'working' command. The answer is a definite yes. I wouldn't actually recommend eating a truffle that was found roadside because of pollution possibilities but such finds don't half make good stories!

The last little nugget I want to recall isn't actually about truffles, it's more about recognising behaviour in your dog. Some things a dog will do naturally, some things must be taught. One lady brought a very nice little cocker spaniel in for training. It did seem to be working to a very high standard but that didn't arouse my curiosity because so many members of the spaniel group absolutely excel at scent work. During a conversation I was talking about how the police use dogs to detect people carrying drugs and the following came out.

Michelle had been in a town centre where the police were doing a drugs search. The police dogs were indicating who smelt of drugs by sitting down in front of them and Michelle's little spaniel Coco started doing exactly the same. A policeman looked across and understandably thought Michelle was part of his team and asked her to check out a group of people that his dogs had already singled out. Michelle was highly amused and replied that she was just passing by... This tale left questions in my mind. "Where did you get this dog?" I asked. When Michelle told me he had needed re-homing and came to her at one year old I then understood where he had been before her. Clearly he had been trained for drugs detection but somehow had managed to fail the course. What a shame, as far as I was concerned his work was brilliant!

MEETING MAZ

Some people don't take any convincing about truffles at all.
They might not have any previous knowledge to any extent
about British truffles but just hearing those words are enough
to send them into orbit.

One lady was reading the local newspaper while she was on
a train. She came across an article about the Dog School
and knew immediately her daughter would love to bring her
dog in for training. The daughter in question was Marion
(Maz) Pennington who promptly rang me up. As it happened
she lived only a couple of miles away but I was just about
to move house to Somerset. It seemed too ridiculous for words
to miss the opportunity so we made urgent plans and Maz
and I met. Maz's young dog was called Seven and he worked
straight through the exercises with no problem at all.
During his breaks I was talking truffle and Maz was talking
cooking. On the enthusiasm stakes I had met my match
and there seemed to be an immense opportunity looming.
Up until that point I had served only very plain truffle dishes
on the special Sunday training group lunches, and in the
home-time goody bags I included some very amateurish
recipe cards, hoping that word about the British truffle would
spread. All of a sudden here was someone who could add
a whole new dimension to what I was doing. Those early few
hours sowed the seeds from which this book has been born.
Please read on to see the results for yourself.

PART TWO:
PREPARING TO COOK YOUR TRUFFLES

A Chef's Delight

Little did I guess, when I decided that the time had come to bring a puppy into the house, that it would lead to a wonderful, mysterious and utterly delicious truffly world. But it has, and it would be terribly selfish not to share the fun and the culinary delights which have followed from this, thanks to my collaboration with Britain's premier truffle hunter, Marion Dean.

If you're reading this book, you're probably already interested in truffles, or dogs, or both. You're probably also amazed that we have truffles in the UK. I know I was. But we do and they're delicious! The recipes in this book have been specifically created for the flavour and texture of our native black Summer Truffles. Better still, each recipe was developed using a truffle found either by my dog, Seven, or Marion's dog, Mufti.

We are led to believe that the price of a truffle falls quite a long way along the scale between somewhat pricey and eye-wateringly expensive. In the case of our black Summer Truffle, this is not necessarily true. The dream scenario is finding your own, but for those needing to buy, you will find some advice from Marion later on, which should come as a pleasant surprise.

An unfortunate result of the high regard in which the truffle is held, and the belief that they are an unaffordable luxury, is that most people are a little afraid of them. Years ago, one Christmas, I bought one of those little jars with a preserved truffle in it, as a stocking filler for my husband. It sat on the shelf for ages while we tried to summon up the nerve, and the inspiration, to do something with it. Inevitably, it ended up past its use-by date and in the bin – what a waste!

So what do you need to know in order to avoid such a tragedy under your own roof?

First, truffles are DELICIOUS, not SCARY! They taste really good, and they make other things taste really good, too.

Second, once you have a truffle in your hand, don't put it on a pedestal, put it in your dinner!

Third, truffles are very simple to cook, and there is a whole string of different recipes coming up, from the really straightforward to the very cheffy. Regardless of how much effort you put into these dishes, the addition of a little fresh truffle will transform them and take them to a higher plane. My advice would be to start off with something simple, in terms both of technical skills and of other flavours. You want the truffle to be the star of the dish at least this first time. Once you've got the hang of it (which you *will* have, in no time at all, I promise), you can get as complicated as you like.

I am here to pass on the results of what has been sheer luxury – the ability to actually *play* with almost unlimited truffles. Whether you are a keen amateur foodie or a professional chef on a tight budget, it is unlikely that you have ever been in that position. Marion has kept the truffles coming, and I have been able to say, "I wonder if..." and then go and find out. I have made your expensive mistakes for you. Although, I have to say, there have been very few – truffles are incredibly versatile and surprisingly forgiving. Perhaps this, coupled with their relative rarity and exquisite taste, is why they remain so very highly prized.

So take the plunge! Don't let the French and Italians have all the fun – it's time for the British truffle to stand up, be counted and fulfil its truffly destiny – to delight the palates of the British people!

Preparation

CLEANING TRUFFLES

Hurrah! You are proudly clutching your truffle and are poised and ready to eat the little beauty. Whether you have found or bought your truffle, if it is fresh it may well still be wearing its mud overcoat. The first thing you will need to do before you can dive in, therefore, is to clean it.

While it may seem perfectly obvious how to clean a truffle when you are sitting reading this, I bet that once you have your truffle in your hand, you will start to experience doubts. Do I run it under a tap, or is it like a mushroom and should simply be dry brushed? How robust is it – am I going to damage it? If I do run it under a tap – hot or cold? Maybe there's some kind of special truffle cleaning agent, ooh, maybe truffle oil... Stop!

Cleaning a truffle is indeed as simple as you think it is before you start thinking about it. Take truffle in hand, run under lukewarm tap water while brushing thoroughly with toothbrush until all traces of dirt are removed.

The black outer coating of the truffle, the peridium, can be quite deeply grooved, so take your time and do be thorough – those grooves and crevices make a lovely hiding place for bits of mud and dirt. It is an identifying feature of the black Summer Truffle that its peridium is firmly attached, unlike, for example, the peridium of the black Winter Truffle (*Tuber brumale*), which is easily removed. You can therefore be quite firm in your handling of the Summer Truffle.

Much as I love truffles, I am not prepared to share a toothbrush with them. They have their own dedicated brush and I would suggest that yours do too!

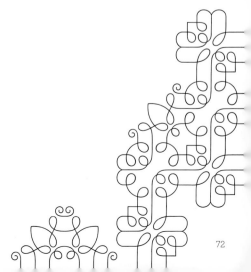

STORING TRUFFLES

The recipe for truffle butter which I give later in the book is a truly excellent way of preserving truffles for anything up to a year in the freezer. However, if you are just looking for a way to keep them in good condition for a couple of days until you cook them, some simple rules should be observed.

I do feel that the truffles need to be able to 'breathe', so do not wrap them in cling film. Choose kitchen paper instead.

The truffles will flavour whatever you store them with. It always seems a great shame to me to squander this magnanimity. So, on the basis that you should never look a gift horse in the mouth, I usually put them straight in with my eggs. Once the truffles and eggs have cohabited overnight, you have truffled eggs, and truffles which, while they have generously imparted flavour to the eggs, have magically not lost any of their own flavour. Another advantage of storing truffles with eggs is that if for any reason you don't have time to clean them straightaway, any mud clinging to the truffle is not going to harm your eggs.

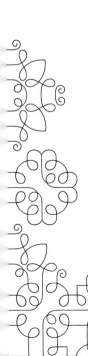

If you have cleaned your truffles straight away, you can get a little more creative about what you store them with. Risotto rice works very well, but I have also stored them in any rice, sugar or pasta, anything which allows some air to get to them and doesn't suffocate them. Just two little considerations. First, make sure the truffles have had the chance to dry off before storing them. Second, if you store your rice, or whatever, in hermetically sealed containers, the truffle may suffer. Check daily. You can transfer a little of your chosen storage medium to a jar, with holes pierced in the lid. Truffles stored this way should keep well in the fridge for up to a week.

Bear in mind, too, that truffles lose moisture day by day. Your truffle is at its biggest and best when fresh.

If you want to use truffles for shavings, do not freeze them. They become spongy and their qualities and inner appearance change. The flavour, however, is quite satisfactorily preserved, so as long as you are preparing a recipe which doesn't require your truffle to be beautifully displayed, shaved across the top, frozen truffles will work well.

It is very important, at this point, to talk about truffle oil.

You may think that slicing up a couple of truffles and dropping them in a bottle of olive oil would be the ideal way both to preserve your truffles, and to make some delicious truffle oil. You would be wrong. This is a potentially dangerous practice. Even if you do see it being recommended on the internet, please do not be tempted. Raw truffle kept in oil could incubate bacteria to dangerous levels. Read on.

If a commercial oil contains small pieces of truffle, these have been processed (cooked) at high temperatures. This makes them safe for storage but has the disadvantage of destroying any flavour or aroma. The flavouring therefore has to be added chemically. Most commercial 'truffle' oils are simply the base oil plus chemical truffle aroma. I have been told that there are some 'real' truffle oils on the market, but as yet I have not been able to find one.

This is not to say that you should avoid truffle oils at all costs. Some of the truffle oils on the market work very well, giving a good truffle flavour at a very affordable price. In lean times, that's not so bad, hey? Be aware, however, that the flavour, while a good imitation, is not the real thing. In layman's terms, it's like comparing a carton of reconstituted orange juice to a juicy, fresh orange. It really is worth giving the genuine article a go, if you possibly can.

When buying and using truffle oil, I would give the following advice:

- Try to buy oil which you have had a chance to smell and taste-this is best done at food shows or in good food halls.

- Buy a small bottle. You really only need a little truffle oil at a time, and if you buy a great big bottle it will not be at its best by the time you approach the second half of it.

- Use sparingly.

- If, having followed this advice, you find that your oil is too strong, decant it to another bottle and dilute with a mild olive oil.

HANDY COOKING APPARATUS

Throughout the following recipes, you will find that truffles seldom go into a dish whole. They tend to be shaved, grated or finely chopped (or 'minced'). This is largely a matter of practicality. If you tried making muscat jelly, for example, with minced truffle rather than grated, I suspect you would end up with all your truffle in the bottom of the glass, rather than marbled evenly through the jelly. However, it is occasionally just a matter of preference, and if you would prefer shavings of truffle in your butter rather than minced truffle, do feel free. However, for the sake of clarity, we felt it would be useful at this point to give you a brief run down of what these terms mean, what tools work well and what the resultant truffles should look like.

SHAVINGS

Truffles are sadly not the most attractive ingredient in the world. Shaving a truffle, however, reveals its exquisite internal marbling and transforms it into a real thing of beauty. When the truffle is shaved, raw, onto the finished dish, this marbling is retained to great effect. Shavings can be made using a number of different methods from scalpels to gorgeous looking metal mandolines. In all honesty, however, the most useful item I have found for shaving truffles is a garlic slicer, such as the one available from Pampered Chef. It effortlessly produces perfectly even shavings of truffle in seconds, and is very handy for temporary storage – i.e., if you don't shave the whole truffle in one dish, you can leave it in the shaver and put it in the fridge until you need it.

GRATED

I recommend a Microplane ® grater for grating truffles. Traditional graters will bruise the truffles as you grate. A Microplane ® grater consists of many individually sharpened blades, and will give you excellent results.

FINELY CHOPPED / MINCED

If you have good knife skills or plenty of spare time, it is not difficult to do this by hand. As I seldom have much (if any) spare time, I have got over a natural aversion to gadgets, and learnt to love my food chopper. Within seconds it will reduce a pile of truffles to a lovely, even, minuscule rubble. I can't find a reason, other than sheer snobbery, not to use it. One piece of advice – when you're sure you have finished mincing truffles for the day, do make sure you remove all traces of truffle from the chopper, using a silicone spatula or similar. That's not a hygiene issue, by the way – I assume you keep your kitchenware clean, and if you don't, it's none of my business! This is purely a 'don't waste any truffle' issue!

Cooking with Truffles

There are a few guidelines to follow when cooking with truffles. Most of these, you will come across as you work your way through the recipes. What it boils down to, though, is don't cook them too hot or for too long. There are, inevitably, exceptions to the rule, but on the whole if you stick to these two guidelines, you can't go too far wrong.

Some of my recipes give formal amounts of truffle in the ingredients lists, and some don't. There are a number of reasons for this, one of which is best illustrated by a brief anecdote.

About 35 years ago, my Dad went to buy the family a proper stereo. This was back in the days when you built your hi-fi element by element. The body of the system having been agreed, the salesman attempted, as he would, to sell Dad some fiendishly expensive speakers.

Dad didn't object to this too much – he was, after all, planning to buy a stereo to last us for a very long time. Plus you can't blame a bloke for trying.

Rather than falling for the spiel, however, Dad simply asked to listen to the same thing through each set of speakers, and when *he* could hear no improvement from one set to the next, he bought the second to last pair he'd listened to. He did not need a flashier set of speakers than that, as any subsequent improvement was lost on him.

I have applied this principle to many purchases over the years – most frequently to wine, it has to be said. There is simply no point in spending money on a speaker more refined than your ear is capable of discerning, or a wine more complex than your palate can appreciate.

This advice is the best I can give you in terms of your truffle usage. For some people, a tiny bit of truffle in a dish will be sufficient to infuse it with a fully rounded truffliness. They are the lucky cheap dates of the truffle world. Others prefer a great deal of truffle.

Equally, you may find that once you get to a certain amount of truffle in a dish, adding more does not make it any trufflier – you have reached your truffle saturation point and your taste buds just can't register any more truffle.

So while I have usually given an idea of the quantity of truffle for each dish, this should always be considered more of a guide than a strict rule. I do think it is a totally individual matter and you really need to determine for yourself how much truffle you like in a dish.

Remember, too, that the truffle in many of the recipes is essentially a seasoning rather than a substantial part of the body of the meal, so adding a little more or less is not going to ruin the dish. Despite the fact that the recipes have been conceived as specifically black Summer Truffle recipes, most of them will work just as well, out of season, with no truffle whatsoever. So don't get hung up on truffle quantities – just go with the flow!

A final bit of general advice: There is an analogy to be drawn between cooking with truffles, and wearing perfume. You can blast a great guff of perfume over yourself so that people for miles around can smell you coming, or you can layer it on gently. A little bath oil, a touch of body lotion and the merest waft of perfume, and you smell subtle but distinct. So it is with truffles. In many instances, it is possible to layer up the truffle flavour in a dish, by truffling your eggs as described above, for example, then adding a little truffle butter somewhere along the way and shaving on some raw truffle right at the end. You will in this way build up a subtle but unmistakable truffly flavour to your dish.

At other times you may just want to hit people over the head with a big truffle hammer – that's fine, too. Just so long as you enjoy it!

So go forth and cook your truffles. And keep these words in the forefront of your mind:

Experiment. Dare. Enjoy.

PART THREE:
COOKING YOUR TRUFFLES

Getting Started

Unless you are a very confident cook, and are also completely familiar with the flavour of truffles, it can be a little daunting to begin cooking with them. This is especially true if you've found them yourself, as found truffles seem even more precious than if you've parted with your hard earned cash.

I would therefore recommend that you try one of the following three recipes for your first foray into the world of cooking your own truffles. In themselves, the recipes are deliberately simple, and the other ingredients are totally familiar, so you will really be able to taste what a difference the truffle makes to the dish. Ingredient quantities are loose because I want you have fun, getting used to discovering how much truffle to use, whilst not worrying about exactly how creamy you ought to like your mushrooms!

I do appreciate, however, that this may make it hard to judge how much truffle you need to buy. As you can see from the picture on p220, one small fresh truffle, weighing as little as 20g, will produce a most satisfactory pile of shavings. This should be sufficient for a good two, possibly three, recipes. Makes it all, suddenly, seem rather more achievable, doesn't it?!

Truffles seem to do something to the flavours around them, and make your taste buds jump around. When I develop a recipe, I tend to make a batch with truffles and a batch without, so that I can tell how much of a difference the truffle has made. This may sound irksome, but it is surprising that the truffled version sometimes doesn't 'taste of truffles' – especially in the case of puddings. When you compare the truffled to the untruffled, however, the difference is always obvious. If you are of an enquiring (or sceptical) mind, you may want to try this too. With many of the recipes, it is possible to get to a certain stage, then simply to put aside a small quantity before you add the truffle, which is frequently the last ingredient, rather than making the whole thing twice.

Once you've had a bash at something simple, the world is your oyster. Or should that be your truffle?

Simple Recipes to Start With

A note, here, before we start. These recipes, as mentioned above, are for dishes with which you will be highly familiar, and I have deliberately left the quantities very loose. I have suggested that you use three eggs per person in your scrambled eggs, but other than that, I haven't been very specific – particularly in the amount of truffle used.

My objectives are:
a) to get you over worrying about cooking with truffles; and
b) to help you to decide how much truffle you like in a dish, by allowing the truffle to shine through.

Scrambled Eggs
with Truffles

This is a famous combination, and everyone knows how to scramble eggs. I do think, however, that it's worth putting down a recipe for it, as when using a rare and precious ingredient such as a truffle one can have a sudden loss of confidence in one's abilities, and need a bit of holdy-handies. Besides, scrambled eggs are so frequently and cheerfully murdered – turned into ghastly grainy or gelatinous heaps sitting resentfully in a puddle of what looks like dishwater. Done as follows, however, they are fit to impress an Empress.

With such a simple recipe, each element must be right. The first element is the pan. I always scramble eggs in a frying pan, skillet or VERY HEAVY wok, never a saucepan. This way you have a larger surface area, the eggs are in better contact with the heat, and can be scrambled more evenly.

So, find the heaviest pan you have and melt the butter over a slow heat. There is no hurry.

Once the butter is melted, break your eggs into the pan (or into a cup first to avoid bits of shell – crunchy scrambled eggs are not a delicacy, even with a forest full of truffles scattered over the top with gay abandon!).

The heat should at this stage be so low that the eggs do not begin to set around the edges. Gradually, turn the heat up until the eggs just begin to set. Keep the pan at this temperature. From here on in, it's just a case of stirring. It takes a while, so be patient – it will be worth it.

Before the eggs set completely, remove from the heat. Be brave and remove them slightly before they're quite how you like them, as they will continue to cook. If you really want to up the luxe-factor, you can stir in a tablespoon of double cream at this point, but it does risk over egging the, er, eggs.

Arrange toast on plates and either pile the scrambled egg on top or on the side, according to preference. Shave the truffles over the eggs and scrunch on the tiniest bit of salt. Take a deep nose full of the smell coming off that plate!

This is a great dish as it comes, but if you're looking to take things up a notch, here are some other delightful variations.

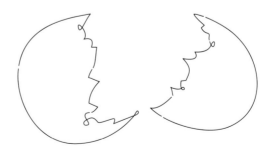

INGREDIENTS

- Generous knob of butter

- Eggs – three per person

- Toast

- Truffles

- Good salt, such as Maldon or Cornish Sea Salt

Scrambled Eggs and Then Some

SMOKED SALMON

Serve with toast and lay slices of smoked salmon, at room temperature, across the warm eggs.

DRY CURED HAM

Replace smoked salmon with slices of British dry-cured ham if you can find a local source. Otherwise, Parma, Serrano or Black Forest hams are perfectly good alternatives.

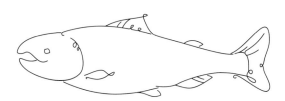

ASPARAGUS

Serve with blanched or griddled asparagus (see recipe for barbecued asparagus on p 111).

MUSHROOMS

Serve with wild mushrooms, lightly sautéed in butter.

Truffled Mushrooms
for One (or two, or many!)

This is the first recipe I made with fresh truffles. Happily, the truffles arrived through the post from Marion just as I sauntered home from a mushroom foraging session in the woods, with a basket full of shaggy parasol mushrooms. This dish is incredibly simple to make, and is just heaven on a plate. I have it for lunch at least three times a week during mushroom season!

Although I wouldn't advise you to go out mushrooming with no experience, do try to get some interesting mushrooms. At the very least, use Portobello or Portobellini rather than cultivated white button mushrooms, which have little or no flavour of their own. There are no quantities given at all below, as I feel that it would be unnecessarily prescriptive of me to tell you that you like too much cream in your mushrooms, or whatever. It's all a matter of taste. However, do go easy on the garlic – you want to be able to taste the truffle!

Melt the butter over a low heat in a large heavy frying pan until it begins to foam. Add the crushed garlic. Slice or tear (I tear!) the mushrooms into bite-sized chunks and add to the pan. Turn over gently to coat in butter, but don't bash them about too much or they will bruise and discolour. Cook them slowly until you can't see any raw areas.

Chop or rip up a handful of flat leaf parsley, including stalks, and add most of it to the pan, along with a twist or two of freshly ground black pepper and a little good quality salt – preferably a pinch of sea salt scrunched between finger and thumb. All this emphasis on tearing and ripping is not a culinary must, it's just that, in my case, anticipation gets the better of me and this is the quickest way to get it all in the pan!

Stir in a tablespoon or so of cream and gently turn the mushrooms to coat. Just before removing it from the pan, shave some truffle into the mushrooms, and gently fold through.

Serve on toast and sprinkle with the remaining parsley and a little salt.

You can of course butter the toast if you like, but I don't think it needs it – this way you can kid yourself that you're being slightly healthier...

As a more impressive alternative, and if you are more patient than me, this is delicious served with grilled chicken breasts and wild rice.

INGREDIENTS

- Knob of butter
- Crushed garlic
- Selection of mushrooms – a good handful or two per person
- Salt
- Black pepper
- Flat leaf parsley
- Cream – whipping, sour, double, fraiche, oat – whatever you have in the fridge
- Fresh truffles sliced or shaved into slivers

Truffled Spaghetti

This is just about the most straightforward thing you can do with a truffle, but ooh, it's delicious! Again, I'm slightly embarrassed to call it a recipe, but it is, after all, just to get you started!

Prepare the spaghetti according to the cooking instructions. Toss through a little olive oil. Grate on the Grana Padano (very similar to Parmesan, but with a milder flavour). Shave over the truffle. Season. Serve. Done.

INGREDIENTS

– Spaghetti – approx. 75-100g dried per person

– Olive oil – to coat

– Grana Padano cheese – to taste

– Truffle

– Salt & pepper

Starters

Whether you are planning a full truffle tasting menu, or just one truffly dish, starters are – well – a good place to start!

I have always found starters to be the most exciting section on a restaurant menu, and my usual approach to eating out is to fancy all the starters, end up ordering two, bypass the main course altogether and pick an entirely luscious pudding (or cheese) if I have space. I suspect they appeal to me because of the opportunity for creativity, despite their relatively small portion. Maybe that in turn is because chefs like to use the starter as a chance to kick your taste buds into action.

Whatever it is, I hope you'll find that these starters do tickle your fancy and pique your curiosity, and that you'll try as many of them as you can!

Hot Truffle Shot

In complete contrast to the first three recipes, this is an unapologetically cheffy dish.

When I dreamt it up, I had very recently been served a White Onion, Parmesan and Coffee Cappuccino which sounded odd but tasted delicious. I decided that something similar, but with a truffle twist, could be equally delicious. It is. Still very simple to prepare, but massively impressive.

I've put it under starters, but I think that if someone was expecting a three course meal, they may feel this was a rather light course! I would, in that case, tend to serve it as what the French call an amuse-bouche (or, more colloquially, an amuse-gueule), with a light starter to follow. If you are deliberately serving a light meal, however, this is an ideal starter. It may be small, but it has enough flavour to satisfy a small regiment. The recipe will make just over a pint, but I would recommend that you not be tempted to serve it to four people as a soup because the flavour is very rich.

The milk should be good full fat Jersey, and the wine should be something you'd happily drink. The ingredients are few, so the quality must be good.

Serves: 8

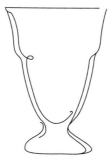

INGREDIENTS

- Knob of butter

- 2 medium sized onions, diced

- ¾ pint of milk

- ½ glass of good dry white wine

- Fresh truffles

- 50g cold butter

Melt the butter over a low to medium heat and toss in the onions. Allow these to sweat down until translucent, but not to colour, or – heaven forfend – burn.

Add the milk and barely simmer for half an hour or so, to allow the milk to really take on the onion flavour. Add the white wine. At this point, the milk will almost certainly curdle. Don't panic! It doesn't matter in the least. Heat back through to barely simmering.

Pour the contents of the pan into a liquidiser or one of those tall receptacles which come with hand held blenders. Blast it thoroughly to purée it until as smooth as possible. You can't do this in the pan with the hand held blender, as you really won't get it sufficiently smooth.

Push the resultant purée through a sieve, using the back of a spoon. You will need to chivvy it around to get it happening. Keep at it until the liquid has all run through and you're left with a residue with pretty much the texture of mashed potatoes. Indeed, if you mash the residue into potatoes, it's delicious – I just hate to throw anything away!

Wash the pan and return the liquid to it. Shave some truffle into the broth. Exactly how much you use is entirely personal taste – the more you use, the stronger it will be. You don't want to lose the truffle flavour by using too little, and it's hard to use too much in this one, in my opinion!

Cover, and allow the warm milky broth and the truffles to sit for a while over a very low heat, to infuse. If preparing ahead for a dinner party, you can leave the broth at this point and return to it just before you are ready to serve it.

Cut the cold butter into cubes and toss into the warm broth one by one, whisking furiously.

Pour into shot glasses or sherry schooners and serve immediately.

-BY THE WAY-

Rather than discarding the residue of the purée, use it to top jacket potatoes, or stir through mashed potatoes, or even spread it on buttered bread! Too good to be forgotten!

Trufflessoise

It's hard not to love leek and potato soup anyway, and if you truffle it, it just gets better. Serve hot on a cold day for a delicious, warming, filling, rib-sticking meal after a long truffle-hunt. Serve cold on a hot day for a refreshing and sophisticated yet rustic meal. All things to all people – truly a winner.

Serves: 4

Melt the butter with the oil over a low heat and add the onions. Cover, and allow the onions to soften for about ten minutes.

Add the leeks and potatoes, and stir to coat with the melted butter and oil.

Add the truffle butter and stir until melted in. Cook for a further ten minutes, still over a low heat, to preserve the full flavour of the truffles.

Add the chicken stock and simmer for 20 minutes.

Blend in a liquidiser or using a hand held blender, until smooth. If you're not too fussy about the smoothness of the texture, you can do this in the pan. If you want to go for the smoothest of the smooth, right up the other end of the scale, you can go to the extent of pushing it through a coarse sieve. Personally, I favour the more rustic approach. Shave in the truffle and allow it to stand.

Either eat while still warm, or chill down in the fridge, but either way, serve with a swirl of cream – double, single, fraiche – entirely up to you! If you like a sprinkle of something for a garnish, a little crisped onion, or some chopped flat leaf parsley along with, of course, a couple of shavings of fresh truffle.

INGREDIENTS

- Knob of butter and slurp of mild oil, such as light olive or rapeseed
- 100g onions, finely chopped
- 175g leeks, finely sliced and washed
- 125g potatoes, finely sliced
- 20g truffle butter (see recipe p191)
- 1 pint chicken stock
- Truffle
- Swirl of cream

Truffled
Scotch Egg

When you are in a recipe-creating mind zone, all sorts of ideas pop into your head. Some of them are frankly ridiculous, but some just feel right the minute you think of them, and you can't work out why everyone doesn't do them. This is one of the latter.

If you don't have a food processor, replace the slices of bread with purchased breadcrumbs, but please, not those horrible orange crunchy ones – something vaguely natural looking. Japanese Panko crumbs are frightfully trendy, so maybe go for those.

I have given sausages as the meaty ingredient in this recipe, as they work really well, and the consistency is perfect for holding together and wrapping around the egg. If, however, you are of an adventurous bent, they also work beautifully if you replace the sausage meat with ground rose veal mixed with a little egg to bind.

Guidelines: if not using a proper deep fat fryer, be clever in your choice of pan size. Too big and you will need an awful lot of oil. Too small and you risk oil splashing about and catching light. Go for a medium pan and enough oil to float the eggs – a couple of inches should be plenty.

Serves: 1 - 6

INGREDIENTS

- 1 dozen quails' eggs

- 500g really good quality sausages, skins removed

- 10g truffle shaved into slivers

- 1 hen's egg

- 3 slices of bread or two English muffins (wheat-free work very well)

- Vegetable or sunflower oil for deep frying

- Truffle

- Swirl of cream

Truffled
Scotch Egg

Place the quails' eggs into a saucepan and add enough boiling water to cover the eggs, plus their height again. Return to the boil and cook the quails' eggs for a minute and a half*, then immediately plunge them into a bowl of ice cold water while you prepare the other ingredients. You need the eggs to be set enough to peel, but sufficiently softly boiled that they still have a little softness there once they've been deep-fried.

Beat the hen's egg and place it into a small bowl or tea cup.

Whizz the bread into crumbs in a food processor and place in a dry frying pan over a low heat to gently toast. Watch like a hawk! You do not want the crumbs coloured, just dried out slightly. Obviously, if you are using ready-made breadcrumbs, you can skip this step.

Place breadcrumbs into a shallow bowl.

Peel quails' eggs, making sure to rinse off any lingering fragments of shell.

Divide sausage into 12 equal balls.

For each quail's egg, take a ball of sausage meat. Take two thirds of the ball and form it into a little cup. Place slivers of truffle inside the cup and pop an egg in. Mould the cup so that it hugs the egg, leaving a gap at the top. Tuck another sliver of truffle in the gap and top off with a hat made of the remaining 1/3 of the ball of sausage meat. Roll lightly between your hands and gently tease any cracks closed.

Dip the ball in the egg and roll it in the crumbs.

Heat the oil in a medium sized pan. If you have a sugar thermometer, use it. The oil should be 150C/300F.

Lower (DON'T drop! Splashing etc.) one single Scotch egg into the oil and fry for two minutes. This should be sufficient to cook the sausage meat through, if the oil is at the correct temperature. After two minutes, remove the egg from the oil and place on kitchen roll. Slice through and check that everything is cooked through as it should be. Assuming that it is, eat the egg. (That's cook's perks.) You can eat these Scotch eggs hot (pretending that they're all slightly over or under done, so nobody else gets any) or serve cold at picnics*. Totally and utterly posh, no?!

-CHEF'S TIP-

If you don't have a sugar thermometer and you find that the meat is over or under cooked, adjust the heat up or down until you find that you get a perfect egg in two minutes. If the oil is too hot, the crust will burn before the meat is cooked through, and if too cool, the crust will not crisp properly.

Being still something of a coward, I never do more than two eggs at a time, and I set a timer at two minute intervals to ensure that I get it absolutely spot on each time. As you may have gathered, I'm usually very relaxed in my approach to cooking, but in this case I feel it is best to play safe.

* Please note, if serving cold the next day, for example at a picnic, you will need to cook the eggs through.

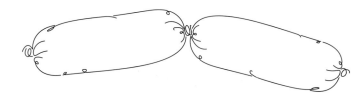

Barbecued Asparagus
with Truffle Mayonnaise

Asparagus and truffle are a lovely combination, and luckily you can get hold of asparagus most of the year, now. If you can get fresh local asparagus to collide in season with truffles, you are, my darlings, laughing. Trust me.

If the weather lets you down, which, let's face it, is more than a remote possibility, you can do the asparagus in a griddle pan on the hob. If you CAN barbecue them, however, it adds a lovely layer of smokiness, which works very well with the mayonnaise.

Serves: 4 as a starter, 2 as a light lunch

Mix together the lemon juice, olive oil, garlic, pepper and salt in a ziplock plastic bag big enough to fit the asparagus in, too.

Remove any woody ends from the asparagus. The best way to do this is to bend the asparagus gently from the tip and move downwards until you find the snapping point.

Add the asparagus to the bag, close it and manipulate to ensure that the asparagus is fully coated. Pop it in the fridge or leave aside to marinate for a couple of hours or overnight.

Barbecue the asparagus in a barbecue basket until slightly blackened in places, but still *al dente*. If using a griddle pan, ensure that it is very hot before you add the asparagus.

Serve hot or cold, with the truffled mayonnaise.

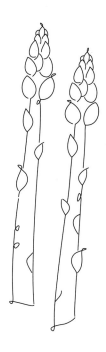

INGREDIENTS

- Juice of half a lemon
- 2 tbsp olive oil
- 1 clove of garlic, finely sliced
- Black pepper
- Salt
- 1 bundle of asparagus
- 1 Quantity of Truffled Mayonnaise
  (see recipe on p193)

Baked Camembert
with Truffles

Being something of a turophile (that's a cheese lover – and yes, I had to look it up!), I've baked Camembert with all manner of things in my time – studded with rosemary and garlic and trickled with a little white wine is good, as is stuffed with walnuts and apple slices, or pecan nuts and cranberries for a November nod to our cousins celebrating Thanksgiving over the pond. But truffles have to top the bill. This is one of those dream recipes with barely any ingredients or preparation required, but, oh my goodness, what a result!

Sacrilegious though it is to suggest, please put the cheese in the fridge for half an hour to 45 minutes before you start – it makes it so much easier to slice and, in this particular case, it will not affect the final flavour in the least!

Serves: 2 - 6

Preheat the oven to 180C/350F.

Remove and discard the paper/plastic in which the cheese is wrapped, but keep the box.

Cut the Camembert across the equator, so you are left with two equal discs. The cheese will have settled slightly in the box, so the bottom disc will be slightly smaller in circumference than the top. The top, in turn, will have spread itself comfortably and muffin-topped its way over the box and into the lid.

Place the bottom disc back in the box and sprinkle as liberally as you dare with shaved truffles. Sprinkle fresh thyme leaves over the truffles. Place the top disc back on top. Place the sides together, rind outwards, so it is back looking pretty much as it did before you started – unless you couldn't bear to put it in the fridge and had 'An Incident' when you tried to slice it!

Place the lid back on the box, put the box on a baking tray (as there is bound to be a little oozing) and bake in the oven for 10 minutes. If you are in any doubt as to whether the box will hold together in the oven, tie some string around it.

Remove from the oven and serve in the box, along with lots of warm, crusty bread and a long stick to beat off intruders, especially if Marion Dean is in the vicinity. In fact, probably safest to make an extra one just for her!

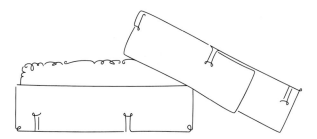

INGREDIENTS

- One standard sized Camembert, in wooden box held together with staples, not glued (or it will come undone in the heat of the oven)

- As much truffle as you can spare

- Fresh thyme

Truffled Hard Boiled
Eggs with Mayo

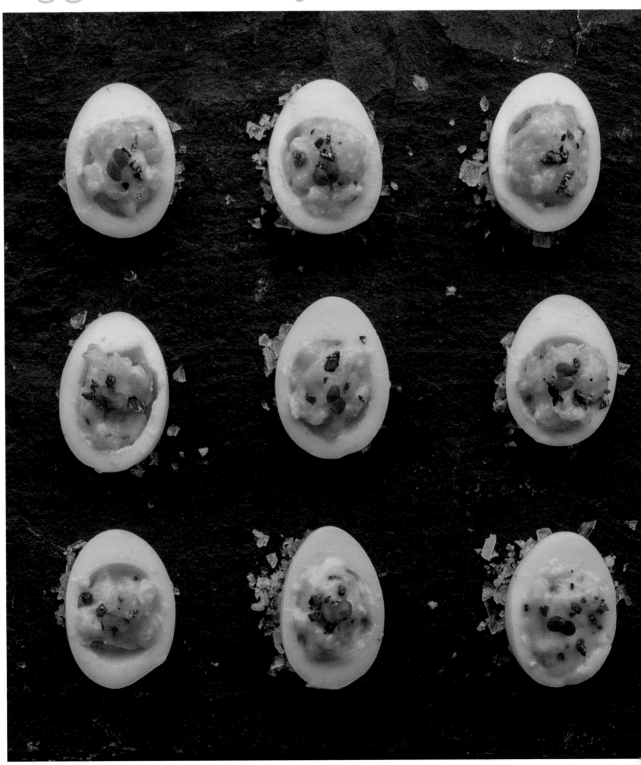

An old 70's favourite, but divine on a picnic, for a bit of alfresco dining, or, if using quails' eggs, as a rather fabulous little canapé.

Hard boil the eggs – timing depends entirely on the size of the eggs, but don't overdo them. As a rule of thumb for hens' eggs, five minutes from coming to the boil to turning off should be sufficient.

Plunge the eggs into ice cold water and allow them to come to room temperature. Please bear in mind that if you leave the eggs in the pan and just run some water on to them, the water will not cool the eggs – the eggs will heat the water. So long as you don't over-boil the eggs, and you do get them into cold water as soon as possible, you will avoid that hideous crime against all things ovate – the Grey Yolk.

Shell the eggs and cut in half. Scoop out the yolks and mix with truffled mayonnaise. Do not attempt this if the yolks are still hot – the mayonnaise will suffer. The amount of yolk to mayo is another one of those judgement calls. It depends entirely how you like them but in principle about two parts yolk to one part mayo will work well.

Return the yolks to their little cavities in the whites. You can either spoon them in or pipe, depending on how fancy you want them to look. If piping, ensure that the mixture is extremely smooth and slightly on the firm side, so that it maintains its shape. If spooning in, please yourself!

A couple of suggestions with this...

As mentioned, quails' eggs will make a very pretty little canapé. For canapé purposes, you can further top these eggs with a dab of caviar, salmon eggs, a shaving of truffle or some fine chives.

If you can get hold of duck eggs, the ratio of yolk to white is very generous...

INGREDIENTS

- Eggs
- Truffled Mayonnaise
  (see recipe on p193)

Light Meals and Lunches

While starters are my favourite things on a restaurant menu, lunches are my favourite things to cook at home.

Lunch can be such a utilitarian meal. How often could you use the phrase, "I just grabbed a sandwich" to describe your lunch? Poor old neglected meal. With a bit of thought, however, it can so easily become the best meal of your day.

The great thing about most lunches is that you usually only have to please yourself, so no compromising on ingredients or diluting flavours. However, if you've come to this book looking for a good lunch recipe, I'm guessing that you're planning to elevate that utilitarian meal to something really out of the ordinary. What a treat! Let's crack on.

Triple Truffled Truffle Omelette for One

This is a lovely, indulgent quick lunch with which to reward yourself for a good morning's truffle hunting – or any other excuse you can think of for a treat!

To 'truffle' your eggs, simply leave them for a couple of hours, or preferably overnight, in a container with some fresh truffles. The porous shells will allow the eggs to take on the flavour of the truffles. The container needn't be airtight – in fact, it shouldn't be or the truffles will tend to 'sweat'. You'll discover that whatever you keep your truffles in will tend to take on the scent, be it eggs, rice, cupboard, or shed!

Melt butter over low heat in small frying pan until foaming but not brown.

Beat the eggs in a large mug and add a small splash of water. Add the eggs to the pan and swirl, keeping the heat low to medium.

When the eggs begin to set, gently push the edges of the omelette inwards and tip the pan to allow the unset egg to trickle out to the clear part of the pan. Repeat.

Add truffle shavings and a tiny sprinkle of truffled salt, and fold in two.

Serve while still moist and slightly runny – or as they say in France, *'baveuse'*.

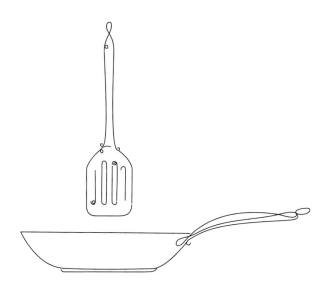

INGREDIENTS

– Generous knob of butter

– Two eggs – truffled

– Water

– Truffle to taste

– Pinch of salt – truffled or regular
  sea salt

"Sev's First Truffle" Cheesecake

I wanted to do something a bit special with the very first truffle that my dog, Seven, found. It was important that this particular truffle be a total star and I wanted to create a dish which I would always connect with this big first! So here it is.

As I was using a single truffle and didn't want it to get lost in the other ingredients, I made a very small cheesecake, using a 12cm loose-bottomed tin. I'll give the quantities for that, and you can multiply them up. For a 20cm tin, for example, you'll need three times as much, and you will need to increase the cooking time accordingly.

Serves: 2 - 4

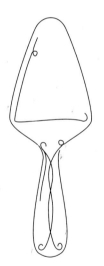

INGREDIENTS

- 70g oatcakes
- 50g butter
- 60g mild spreadable goats' cheese
- 110g full fat cream cheese
- 1 egg
- 30g mild Cheshire cheese
- 20-30g fresh truffle
- 6 or 7 sprigs fresh thyme
- 1tbsp Dove's Farm wheat-free plain white flour
- 2tbsp double cream
- 1 egg white

Preheat the oven to 170C/340F.

Blitz the oatcakes in a food processor, melt the butter, and combine. Press into the bottom of the tin firmly, and place in the fridge to set.

Add the first two cheeses and the egg to the clean food processor bowl and blend until smooth. Grate in the Cheshire cheese using a medium grade Microplane ® grater, and shave the truffle into the mixture.

Pick the leaves off the thyme sprigs and add to the mix, reserving a few for garnishing. Add the flour and cream and stir gently together.

Whisk the egg white until light and frothy – you know the trick. When you can turn the bowl upside down over someone's head (or your own, if you're feeling brave!) and it leaves them un-egged, they're done.

Fold the egg white into the cheese mixture so that it is evenly combined, but not so enthusiastically as to knock all the air out of the egg white.

Remove the base from the fridge and spoon the cheese mixture over it. Level the surface with the back of a spatula.

Place in the oven and cook for 30 minutes. As you remove it from the oven, check that it is set by shaking gently. There should not be too much movement in the centre of the cake. Resist the urge, however, to cook it until there's no movement or give whatsoever, or you will end up with a kind of large, rubber hockey puck!

Allow to cool before serving, garnished with the remaining thyme sprigs. Serve with salad.

Goats' Cheese
with Truffled Honey

I 'discovered' goats' cheese on a family holiday to France, aged about eight. It was served everywhere, grilled on little croutes with crisp salads around it, drizzled with herbed olive oil, or slathered with rich, pungent honey and studded with thyme. My love of goats' cheese has stayed with me ever since, and if it appears on a menu in any form, I find it very difficult indeed not to order it. Coupled with the truffled honey here, it is just wonderful. If you can't get hold of truffled honey, you can use any runny honey (preferably thyme, though) and place a couple of slivers of truffle on the toast under the cheese just before it goes under the grill.

Serves: 2

Warm the olive oil and pick the thyme leaves into it. If the thyme was picked several days ago and is beginning to dry out, this is easier as you can just roll the sprigs between your hands to release the leaves. Allow this to steep for several hours or overnight.

Toast the bread on one side.

If using a roundel of cheese such as Gevrik, cut the top and bottom rinds off the goats' cheese, but leave the edge rinds on, and cut the remainder in half through the equator. Otherwise, if using a log of cheese, simply cut into ½ inch slices.

Drizzle the herbed olive oil onto the untoasted side of the bread and place the cheese on top. Spoon the truffled honey over the cheese in a swirl.

Place under the grill until beginning to colour. Garnish with a small sprig of fresh thyme and serve with a handful of dressed rocket leaves.

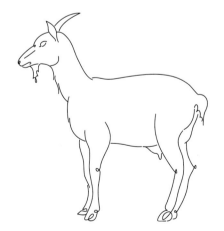

INGREDIENTS

- 60ml olive oil

- Several sprigs of thyme

- Half an English muffin per person, or one muffin-sized slice of good bread

- Goats' cheese – one small roundel of rinded cheese, such as Gevrik, or if using a log such as Soignon, 1 inch

- 2 tsp truffled honey

- 2tbsp double cream

Totally Truffled Poached Eggs on Crumpets

The best breakfast ever. I frequently have it for lunch, too. And dinner, actually, if I'm home alone. Just writing this recipe is making my fingers itch to go and cook it!

This is a perfect example of layering the flavours – just a little bit here and there builds a lovely truffly flavour throughout the dish.

Oh, and there are a list of truffly options at the end of this, so please make sure you read the recipe in full before you either do your shopping, your preparation, or you actually start cooking it!

Serves: 1

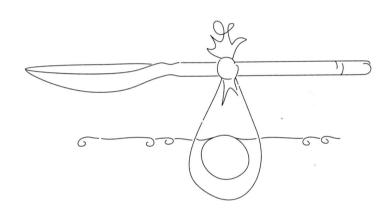

INGREDIENTS

- Very fresh free range egg
- A little oil
- Thyme
- Black pepper
- Crumpet
- Butter
- Salt

Totally Truffled Poached Eggs on Crumpets

If your eggs have been laid today, they will probably poach just fine in the normal way – bring water to the boil, lower the heat, swirl, drop in the egg and leave until poached. However, as eggs age, although still perfectly fine for eating, the whites lose their viscosity, which is why it is very hard to poach week-old eggs. You get froth, and wisps, and a pan full of mess. SO, if you're not sure how old your eggs are, or if you are a little nervous about poaching eggs – especially if you're doing lots at a time – try this foolproof method.

Line a teacup or similar with cling film, lightly oil and sprinkle in a few fresh thyme leaves and a little black pepper, which gives a lovely mottled effect. Break an egg into the lined cup. Gather the cling film together so the egg is contained in a little sack, with the oil, thyme and pepper. Bring a pan of water to the boil and lower the heat. Lower the egg into the water and place a wooden spoon across the pan horizontally. Wind the cling film over the spoon to support the egg. Cook for four to five minutes.

Meanwhile, toast a crumpet and butter it. Usually, I wouldn't dream of telling you what type of butter to use, but in this case it should be unsalted because… Sprinkle the buttered crumpet with a pinch of sea salt.

Remove the egg from the pan and from the cling film. Place on the crumpet and garnish with some little sprigs of fresh thyme. So, the astute reader will have noticed that there is no truffle in this recipe! That's because you can do any or all of the following, depending on what truffles and truffly things you have to hand. I have actually done all of them in one go. The result was wonderful, and surprisingly not overpowering in the least.

Starting from the beginning, if using the cling film method, which I highly recommend, you can brush the cling film with a little truffle oil.

Before you add the egg, using the cling film method, you can shave a couple of slivers of truffle into the prepared cling film.

Use truffled eggs.

Butter the crumpet with truffle butter.

Sprinkle the buttered crumpet with truffle salt rather than plain sea salt.

Shave some fresh truffle over the finished dish before serving.

So go truffling berserk, and I hope you enjoy this one as much as I do.

Marion Dean has been kind enough to assert that my technique of adding small amounts of truffle in 'layers' or stages is worthy of an honour for services to the culinary arts. I couldn't possibly be so immodest as to agree – but you really owe it to yourself to try it!

Steamed Truffles
in Piggy Jackets

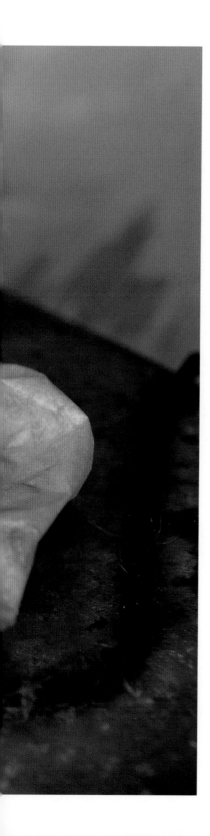

This is strictly a recipe for when you have OODLES of spare truffles, as is CinderTruffella. You can give four people a very good taste of truffle with one truffle finely sliced over something delicious. Or you can give one person a single truffle and leave them hungry... However, it is very delicious, and worth it in times of plenty.

Wrap the truffle in the bacon, trimming it so you have a single layer of bacon all 'round.

Wrap the baconed truffle in the paper.

Tie it up with the string.

Steam for 40 minutes.

Unwrap and eat!

INGREDIENTS

- Truffles – however many you are prepared to use!

- Very thinly sliced streaky bacon – about half a slice per truffle, but this will depend on the size of the truffle!

- Greaseproof paper, or the paper from a pat of butter

- String

CinderTruffela

Marion Dean happened across a vague mention of these in a 19th century paper by the Reverend M J Berkeley (fascinating man – worth Googling). Recipes in general were not written in the form they now are, and Reverends are still not necessarily known for their skill in recipe writing, so a vague mention was really all we got. However, not to be disheartened where truffles are concerned, we decided that the only thing for it was to experiment, donned our white coats and hairnets (no, not really hairnets...), and got stuck in!

Serves: 2

When the fire is out but the ashes are still very much glowing, place the truffles on the warmest part you can reach without burning your fingers.

You need to use some common sense, here, because you really don't want to burn the truffles, but nor do you just want to warm them through, so find a bit that is hot but not burning.

Leave the truffles in the fire (I know! Yes, it IS a bit scary the first time!) for approximately 30 to 45 minutes, then remove and eat! I found these delicious, as the fire had imparted its smokiness to them and crisped up the skins, leaving the inside firm but yielding. Mmmm. And if you're about to go for a walk, you can wrap them in foil and hold them in your pockets to warm your hands up, then eat them before they get cold. These have to be the fanciest hand warmers out there, I think?

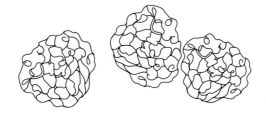

YOU WILL NEED

- Truffles

- Log fire

Truffled Potato Chutney Cakes with Poached Egg

When I made the final version of the Truffled Potato Chutney (see recipe, p199), I wasn't making it for a specific meal or event. I also made double the quantity I've given in that recipe, although only half of it was truffled. As you can imagine, I had a considerable amount left over, and had to find a use for it. This is a bit of an occupational hazard when writing a cookbook, so it wasn't the first time this had happened, but I'm almost 100% certain that this is my favourite result. Sadly, it's unlikely you'll have much chutney left over. Ah, you're right. You can indeed make it especially for this dish!

Serves: 2

As a starter, allow one egg per person, but this would make a very satisfactory lunch in a double quantity, with a bit of salad on the side. Surprisingly, it's equally delicious with a nice cold glass of Sauvignon Blanc or a robust Cotes du Rhone.

Allow approximately 150g of chutney per egg, and use chutney straight from the fridge.

Shape the chutney into a tall cake, a little smaller than a crumpet and about twice the thickness. Either use your hands or, for uniformity (and a more formal look), a ring.

Melt a generous knob of butter in a frying pan, turn the heat up, and work quickly. The potato cake must be cool, or it will just fall apart in the pan. Place the cake in the pan and fry for a minute on each side, turning carefully.

Remove from the pan and top with a poached egg – either plain, or Totally Truffled (see recipe, p125).

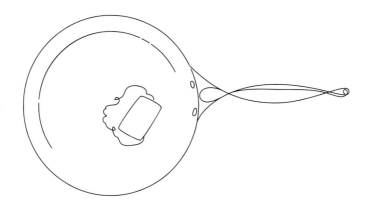

INGREDIENTS
– See Truffle Potatoe Chutney p199
– See Totally Truffled Poached Eggs p125

Posh Up
Your Picnic

There's something about a picnic, isn't there? Whether it consists of a slightly squashed jam sandwich and a flask of squash or a meticulously planned Glyndebourne banquet in a hamper, food seems to taste better in the great outdoors. And I don't think it matters how old you are – the opening, unwrapping and laying out of the delicacies is exciting every time.

So, a truffly picnic, eh? I know, it got me rubbing my hands together, too! All I'm going to do, here, is give you a list of the recipes in this book which would be suitable to take on a picnic. I'm absolutely not suggesting you take everything on the list – lawks, dear! Truffle overkill, if such a thing were possible. It is. It's difficult, but it can be done!

Anyway – pack your picnic as you will, and add a couple of the following dishes to it – you'll be the poshest picnicker in the park!

Do please bear in mind that, with any picnic, there is a risk of the food sitting around in warm conditions (hopefully!) for a while. This is why you should, for example, add your truffle to your vinaigrette later rather than sooner!

PICNIC OPTIONS

- Trufflessoise
- Truffled Scotch Eggs (hard-boil your quails' eggs if making a day in advance)
- Hard-boiled Eggs with Mayonnaise (probably best to assemble these in situ to keep them looking at their best!)
- "Sev's First Truffle" Cheesecake
- Truffled Potato Chutney (made fresh that morning)
- Spanish Omelette
- Sole Tian
- Truffled Honey Cakes (without the syllabub, probably – just a bit easier, and still delicious)
- Mayonnaise (either in sandwiches, or served with cold roast chicken or poached salmon)
- Truffled Potato Salad
- Vinaigrettes (add truffle in situ)
- Vickie's Truffle Cheese (see p203 stockists)

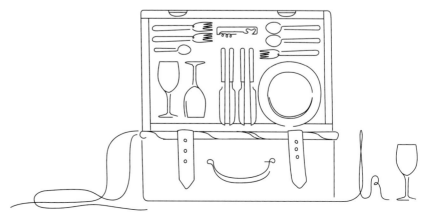

Main Courses

Main courses, as the name suggests, are the main event of the meal – the star of the piece.

For myself, I occasionally find that main courses leave me full but somehow not entirely satisfied. I think this is sometimes due to a triumph of portion size over flavour content – i.e. there's a lot of it, but it's a bit bland.

Enter the truffle...

Back at the beginning of the last century, a Japanese scientist by the name of Dr. Kikunae Ikeda began a series of investigations into the nature of deliciousness. What he discovered was umami – literally meaning 'delicious taste'. He argued that it was a separate taste, distinct from the four accepted tastes of sweet, salt, sour and bitter. For the best part of 80 years or so, a lot of other scientists argued about this, too. However, in the mid 80s, it was finally generally accepted that umami is 'the fifth taste'. Culinary history shows that, although they were unaware of the science of it, ancient Romans actively sought out food combinations high in umami, as did the great Escoffier himself. Apart from its (by definition) deliciousness, umami also has the effect of really rounding out the flavours in a dish, and balancing it.

So you're not going to be surprised, then, are you, when I tell you that truffles have umami. In SPADES!

Pairing
with Wine

There's nothing like a good wine to enhance a good truffle. We know, we've selflessly experimented at length! So for this section, we called in a trusted connoisseur. Earlier in the book, Marion mentioned the Truffle Championship Dog Show and spoke fondly of the generous support given by Forbury's Restaurant and Wine Bar of Reading. There she met Xavier Le-Bellego, proprietor and well-known wine sommelier. Again Xavier has kindly stepped forward to help and we do hope you will apply his advice on choosing a wine to give your meal that finishing touch.

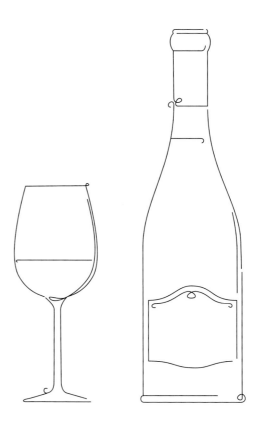

"TRUFFLES LOVE FLIRTING WITH WINES."

To find the perfect match, you'll first need to think about whether your dish is hot or cold, and which is the key component: fish, meat or pasta. It's also a good idea to choose a wine from an area with a similar terroir to that of your truffles, so that your pair will share some common interests. Best steer clear of Champagne as fizz will distract from the delicate flavours of the truffle.

CHICKEN OR COLD DISHES SPRINKLED WITH FRESH TRUFFLE

Here I'd recommend a rich white wine, such as Meursault, Puligny-Montrachet, Crozes-Hermitage Blanc or even an old Sauternes style of wine, as it will embellish the flavour of the truffle. You'll need to combine both texture and aromas rather than pitching them against each other. Be sure only to use a quality wine with a black diamond.

Recommended dishes:
Chicken Septimus
Chicken Ballotine

FISH DISHES AND PASTAS

When it comes hot fish, sea food, pasta or risotto, aim for something lighter. Choose this path as the full flavour or the truffle will be enhanced by the food and brought out by the light notes of the wine. I recommend Chablis, White Châteauneuf-du-Pape, White Corbières or Bergerac.

Recommended dishes:
Pan-Seared Salmon with Truffle Cream Sauce
Pan Fried Scallops with Truffle Squash Sauce and Crispy Prosciutto
Wild Mushrooms and Truffle Risotto

MEAT DISHES

With a hot meat dish, you can still enjoy a rich white wine, or bring out the reds. I love a mature Bordeaux, a Burgundy or any other strong character from the South West of France.

Recommended Dishes:
Venison Wellington

Your sommelier,
Xavier Le-Bellego HND

Proprietor, Forbury's Restaurant & Wine Bar
Reading, Berkshire

Thank you so much Xavier. It is wonderful to have someone who so obviously understands both truffles and wines for this expert advice.

Wild Mushroom
and Truffle Risotto

This is just a classic dish, frequently on the menu in good restaurants. As with many great Italian recipes, there are few ingredients. Again, therefore, make sure that these few things are good – a finished dish can be only as good as its worst component part. I always substitute approximately half the amount of rice in my risottos for celeriac. It keeps the risotto light and fresh, and the nuttiness of the celeriac, in this dish, compliments the truffle very nicely. The following quantity will serve 2-3 people – as usual, multiply for as many as you like!

Serves: 2 - 3

INGREDIENTS

- Fist sized piece of celeriac
- Large knob of butter
- Medium onion, finely chopped
- Two cupped handfuls of carnaroli risotto rice
- 1 glass white wine
- Good chicken stock - approx 750ml, but better to have too much and have some left over
- Olive oil
- 200g mushrooms, wild if possible, and a mixture of types is best
- Parmesan to taste
- Flat leaf parsley
- Fresh Truffle

Chop the celeriac into rice-sized pieces. You can do this entirely by hand, partly by mandolin, or using a food chopper – whichever you prefer. I used to do it by hand, but always use a food chopper now. Life is too short to hand-craft celeriac into grains of rice!

Melt the butter over a medium heat and add the chopped onion. Cook through slowly until transparent.

Add the rice. Stir to coat thoroughly with the melted butter. Now watch the rice – the Italians say it should scream, and the more often you cook risotto the more you'll begin to understand what they mean. Basically, before it begins to colour, but just when you think it may start to, add the glass of white wine. Refill the glass for yourself – there's a lot of stirring coming up!

Stir gently over the same medium to low heat. When the rice has absorbed the wine, and your spoon leaves a clear trail when dragged through the rice, add a ladleful of stock. Repeat stirring, trailing and ladling until the rice is cooked through but retains a little bite – but no crunch! You will have to taste it to determine this. Add the chopped celeriac and one last ladle of stock, stir in and turn the heat down to low.

In a separate pan, heat the oil over a medium/high flame and lightly sauté the mushrooms, seasoning with a little black pepper.

Check that the rice and celeriac have absorbed all of the stock but that it is still moist and has good movement – it shouldn't have turned to cement. Grate in the parmesan. The amount is entirely down to taste – my husband demands none, for me it's lots.

Gently fold in the mushrooms and test for seasoning. How much salt you add at this point depends on how much parmesan you've added and how salty your stock was.

Transfer to bowls and sprinkle with chopped parsley. Shave some fresh truffle over and eat *con gusto!*

Mushroom Pasta

This is a really enjoyable, easy dinner for two people. It's a good way to showcase a truffle, too, without doing anything complicated. As with most of the recipes given here, it does work perfectly well without any truffles, but the truffle certainly gives it that little extra something.

Serves: 2

Cook the pasta according to the instructions, and while it is boiling away...

Melt butter and oil in a pan, gently.

Add mushrooms and coat in butter and oil, turning over gently until cooked through. They should be gently golden but not turning dark and letting off inky juice!

When cooked to your satisfaction, add a squeeze of lemon, a splash of brandy and a tablespoon of cream, and remove from the heat.

Drain the pasta, but don't be too compulsive about it – pasta with a little of the starchy water still hidden in its folds is much silkier and tastier than pasta which has been drained to within an inch of its life and has begun to hint that it may soon become rubbery. It also enables the sauce to coat everything more easily. Add the pasta to the sauce and stir in thoroughly but with a light touch – you don't want to kill it.

Spoon into bowls, shave the truffle over the warm pasta and sprinkle with a little chopped parsley.

INGREDIENTS

– Knob of butter

– Dash of olive oil

– 300g mushrooms – anything with a bit of flavour, so not white cultivated baby buttons

– Half a lemon

– Splash of brandy

– Tablespoon of cream

– 15g truffle

– Flat leaf parsley to garnish

– 150-200g dried pasta

Chicken
Septimus

This was another recipe from one of Sev's early finds. It's very quick and easy to do, but looks quite clever. It's therefore a good, versatile recipe to do either for an impressive dinner party dish, or for a slightly-more-special-than-beans-on-toast dinner at home. Quantities here are for two people, as it seemed a little sad if you're cooking for one or two to have to divide everything by six. Much more cheerful to have to multiply for guests, don't you think?

Serves: 2

Preheat the oven to 180C/350F.

Lay the slices of Parma ham side by side on a board, overlapping. Spread with cream cheese and sprinkle generously with slivers of truffle.

Lay chicken breast across the ham and wrap the ham around the chicken breast, to form a ham envelope enclosing the cheese, truffle and chicken.

Bake in the oven for 20 to 25 minutes, neat side up.

Remove from the oven and slice through diagonally (this has the dual benefit of looking nice and cheffy, and allowing you to check that the chicken is cooked before you serve it – all ovens vary, after all!).

Serve with wild rice, tenderstem broccoli and sautéed wild mushrooms.

INGREDIENTS

- 4 slices of Parma ham
- 100g cream cheese or mildest spreadable goats' cheese
- 20g truffles
- 2 chicken breast fillets

Truffled Ballotine
of Chicken

Okay, so Ballotine doesn't sound particularly British. You have my full permission to refer to it as *Truffled Chicken Parcels*, if it makes you feel better!

Like the above recipe, this is far easier to do than the finished dish would suggest. There is, however, slightly more messing about with this one, and there's no doubt that it is impressive enough to serve to guests.

I wanted to do something that had a bit of a sense of Chicken Kiev about it – delicious and rather exciting to cut into, with all the oozing and hidden flavour – but without the crumbs and the slight inherent naffness (sorry, Chicken Kiev!). Again, quantities are listed for two, but multiply for multiples!

Serves: 2

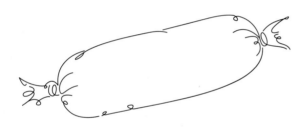

INGREDIENTS

– 2 chicken breasts

– Truffle to taste

– 2 finger-sized pieces of mild Brie

– Thyme

– Salt and pepper

– 6 slices of Parma ham

Truffled Ballotine
of Chicken

Cut into the chicken breast to flatten it out. Depending on the individual breast, sometimes this means a single cut opened straight out like a greetings card, and sometimes two cuts from the centre outwards, opening up like window shutters. Once you have got the breast looking flattish, give it a few whacks with a meat hammer (flat side) or rolling pin wrapped in cling-film, just to even it out a little more.

Shave half the truffles over the chicken breasts, keeping them towards the centre of the breast. Place the cheese in the centre of the chicken breast, lengthways along the grain of the meat. Season, then grate the remaining truffle over the cheese using a medium grade Microplane® grater.

Place 3 slices of Parma ham on a large piece of cling film. Fold the chicken sides in to cover the filling and place on the Parma ham, neat side up. Roll into a cling film sausage, making sure the ends are secure. If in any doubt, tie a little knot in each end. You really don't want the juices leaking out or the water leaking in!

Place the parcels side by side in a saucepan. Cover with boiling water. Return to the boil and turn down to a simmer for 10-12 minutes. Remove the rolls from the water and allow to rest for a couple of minutes, then unwrap and serve with Truffled Mashed Potatoes and griddled asparagus.

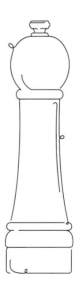

Venison Wellington

There are many stories about the naming of this dish. I had always believed it to be the Duke of Wellington's favourite dish, and to have been served to him before the Battle of Waterloo, but there is little or no evidence supporting this! How disappointing. Other theories are that it resembles a wellie boot (hum, not if you do it right, I would suggest) and that it was invented for a civic reception in Wellington, New Zealand. The truth is lost in the mists of time, but it remains a splendid dish. I have replaced the beef with venison, here, in a spirit of marrying wild foods, but it would work equally well with beef. I would tend to buy puff pastry – I never have the time or inclination to make my own, but please don't let me stop you if the urge takes you!

Please note, if you do not like your meat very rare, take care to choose a slimmer piece of meat. The cooking time is dictated by the pastry, so if you like your meat very well done, this may not be the recipe for you. In this case, it is possible to cut the meat into portions, or use venison fillet steaks before you begin, and make individual Wellingtons. This looks very pretty, but I never do it as I like my meat blue!

Serves: 6

INGREDIENTS

- 1 block of puff pastry
- Glass of red wine
- 350g haunch of venison
- Knob of butter
- 2 shallots
- 2 large flat mushrooms, such as Portabello
- Splash of Madeira
- 150g *foie gras*
- 30g truffle

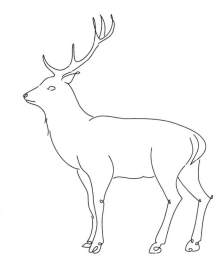

Venison Wellington

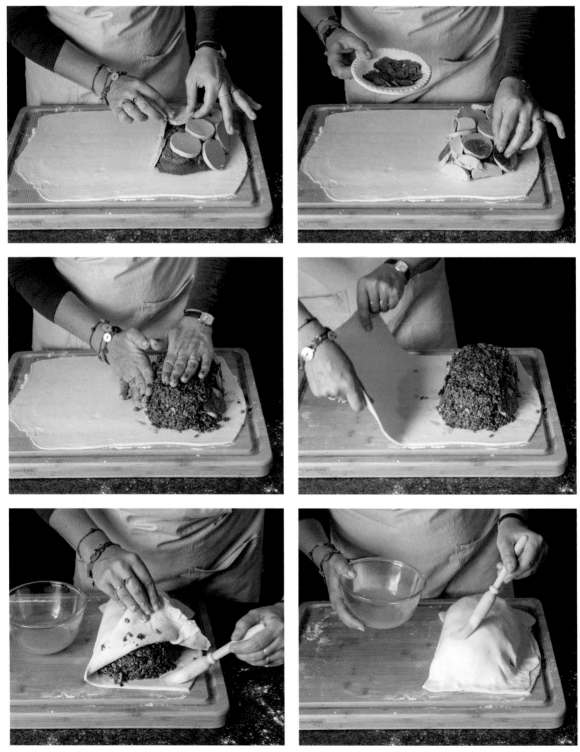

Place the wine and venison fillet in a bag to marinate for several hours.

Sear venison in a hot pan to seal in the juices, then allow to cool thoroughly.

Preheat the oven to 200C/390F.

Chop shallots and mushrooms to a fine dice. Heat butter in a pan until foaming but not browning. Add shallots and turn until translucent. Add mushrooms and a small splash of Madeira and cook through, for approximately 3 minutes.

Roll the pastry out into a rectangle, ensuring that the thickness is between three and five millimetres. A really good way to do this, if you are not used to rolling out pastry, is to place two large thin books (Tintin is ideal) either side of the pastry, so that the ends of your rolling pin sit on the books. This stops you from rolling it out too thin, or too unevenly.

Place the fillet slightly in from one of the short edges, allowing enough of a pastry margin to seal the edges.

Cut your *foie gras* into slices 5mm thick and press onto the exposed sides of the fillet. Coat the *foie gras* in truffle shavings and gently press into place. Spread the mushroom and shallot mixture over the truffle layer, taking care not to dislodge the truffles.

Wrap the pastry over your beautiful creation and seal the edges. Decorate, if desired, and brush with egg wash.

Place in the oven for 25 minutes

Allow to rest for five to ten minutes before serving.

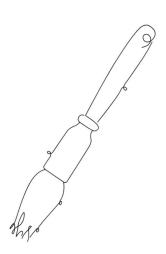

Spanish Style Omelette
(emphasis on the ish)

I find that although I like a little Spanish omelette as an accompaniment to other dishes, it is not my favourite – it can be a little bland for my taste, and I wouldn't want to make a meal of it. With the addition of a truffle, however, the eggs and potatoes take on all the majesty of that little ingredient, and I find I can eat a lot of it. Probably too much, if I'm not careful!

As the methods of producing the Spanish omelette are as fiercely argued as those of the Cornish pasty, my sincere apologies to any Spanish people if the method is not truly as it should be – hence the (rather cowardly) Spanish-'style' disclaimer in the title!

Serves: 2 as a main, or up to 6 as a starter or side dish

Scrub the potatoes and thinly slice, using a mandoline if you have one. Otherwise, just do the best you can with a knife – it will be fine, your tongue won't mind! I never peel potatoes, and wouldn't for this recipe, but if you'd like to, please do.

Slice the onion into rings.

Heat a good glug of olive oil in a pan over a low to medium heat. Add the potatoes and onions and stew in the olive oil for about 25 minutes, stirring occasionally. This is why waxy potatoes work better – with floury ones, you'd risk having mash at this stage.

Strain the potatoes and onions through a colander, reserving the oil. Try to remember not to strain it straight down the sink!

Beat the eggs lightly in a bowl, just to combine the eggs and yolks, and add a little salt and white pepper.

Add the potato and onion mixture to the eggs in the bowl.

Heat a little of the reserved oil in the pan, again over a low to medium heat, and add the egg mixture. Shave over some truffle and bury the slivers amongst the potatoes – you don't want all of the truffle to be either on the surface of the omelette or in contact with the pan.

Once the omelette has set sufficiently, you can have a go at flipping it, keeping it in one piece. If this is a little daunting, you can place the pan in an oven, preheated to 140C/280F, for five to ten minutes or until set.

Serve, cut into slices, and garnished with a little chopped flat leaf parsley if desired.

INGREDIENTS

- 450g medium sized potatoes, waxy to all-purpose is better than floury, just this once!

- 1 large white onion – a sweet Spanish one if you can get one

- Olive oil

- Salt

- 6 eggs

- 15-20g truffle

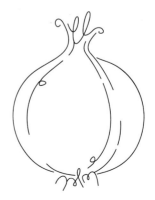

Salmon with Truffle Cream Sauce

This is a delicious sauce with salmon. The recipe here comfortably serves two people, with enough left over to stir into sautéed mushrooms, served on hot toast, for an outrageously indulgent breakfast the next day. Before we start, here are some handy pointers.

I use banana shallots as they are easily available – peeling and finely chopping one banana shallot is quicker and less fiddly than doing the same for three standard shallots. But if you can't get banana shallots, normal ones will be absolutely fine.

Truffle Cream Sauce also partners very well with chicken and game. If you're using with chicken, chop a little tarragon in just before serving. Enjoy!

Serves: 2

INGREDIENTS

- 1 banana shallot or three standard shallots
- Very generous knob of butter
- 1 glass of good white wine
- Finely chopped truffle
- 200ml double cream
- Salt & pepper
- 2 salmon fillets

Peel and finely chop the shallot.

Melt the butter in a saucepan and add the shallot. Sauté gently until soft and translucent, then add the wine.

Simmer very gently until reduced by half.

Add minced truffle.

Stir over medium heat for a couple of minutes.

Add 200ml double cream and season with salt and pepper.

Heat a little oil in a good non-stick pan. When the pan is very hot, place the salmon, presentation side down, in the pan to sear. Turn the heat down to medium and watch the opacity creep up the side of the fillet. When it is 1/4 to 1/3 of the way up the thick end of the fillet, turn the salmon over and remove from the heat. Leave to stand in the pan for 3 or 4 minutes. The centre of the fish should be slightly under done, pink and juicy.

Serve the salmon, generously slathered with sauce, alongside basmati rice and steamed asparagus, or other seasonal vegetable.

A NOTE ON SALMON:

Try to get good fresh salmon from a reputable source. Although salmon is widely available and very affordable now, it is worth paying a bit more for a fine fish. It's noticeably better.

Many towns, however, don't have a dedicated fishmonger any more, so I appreciate that it can be hard to get hold of. I can highly recommend Pengelly's of Looe, in Cornwall. Looe fish is highly prized as the harbour is dry at low tide, leaving the fisherman a small window of opportunity. They have to leave at high tide and return, with their catch, at the following high tide. This means that the fish on the market is as fresh as it can get. Pengelly's, being right on the quay, bang next door to the fish market, really reaps the benefit of this. Their mail order service guarantees delivery within 24 hours to your door.

Sole Tian

It's been nearly 20 years since I've been able to eat wheat, which, as you would correctly imagine, can present problems to the keen cook (and equally keen eater). The up-side, however, is that it forces you to be inventive. Many years ago I saw a recipe for a Provençale tian – the closest thing I can describe it as is a quiche, but with no pastry! Ah yes, mes amis – you may understand that this idea got squirrelled away in one of the many back-rooms of my brain, ready to pop its head around the door again at a then unforeseen time. That time is now!

You will need a good, heavy earthenware or stoneware dish. Traditionally these are glazed on the inside, but in my experience a well-seasoned unglazed dish will work better.

This amount will serve 4-6 people, depending on how hungry they are.

Serves: 4 – 6

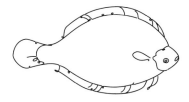

INGREDIENTS

- Garlic clove
- Olive oil
- 5 or 6 eggs, lightly beaten
- 2 generous tbsp of grated pecorino (or other strong hard cheese)
- 3 tbsp crème fraiche
- 150ml full fat milk
- A little nutmeg, freshly grated – really, just a little
- Salt & pepper
- Handful of asparagus spears
- 3 fillets of sole
- A little flour for dusting
- A small truffle

Preheat your oven to 180C/350F.

Cut the garlic clove in half and rub it all over the inside of the dish, then rub with a little olive oil. Enough to stop the contents from sticking, but not so much that they end up sitting in a pool of oil.

Mix together the eggs, cheese, cream and milk.

Cut the asparagus into inch lengths (just for ease of eating) and toss them into the dish. Cut the sole into bite-sized pieces – no more than ½ an inch cubes – and pat them as dry as possible with kitchen roll. Dust with flour.

Arrange in the dish so that each slice will get a reasonably fair share of both asparagus and sole – after all, you don't want any fights breaking out at the table! If you leave the pieces of sole too large, they will also tend to produce extra liquid when cooked, potentially leaving you with the occasional watery pocket. This is not the end of the world, as you can pour it off, but it is far from ideal. So cut them small!

Gently pour the egg mixture into the dish and season with the nutmeg, salt and pepper.

Shave the truffle over the dish (being similarly scrupulous with your sharing) and push the pieces under the surface of the mixture, so that they don't simply dry out on top. The reason for adding them at this stage rather than with the asparagus is that you really do risk them all getting carried off to one little area with the egg, if you do that.

Place the dish in the oven and bake for 20 minutes or so, removing while the centre is still quivering. It will continue to set as it cools, so make sure you don't overcook it, as you really don't want to end up with a rubber Frisbee, when what you should end up with is so many miles from that.

Serve warm but not hot, with a green salad and fresh, crusty bread.

N.B. This is one of those recipes which is ideal when you have an unexpected guest or two, and can't work out how to make your planned three fillets of fish feed four or five people.

Scallops with Truffled Squash Sauce and Prosciutto Crisps

Scallops, fresh from the sea – ahhhh! Surely there can be no finer dish than pan-fried scallops, so fresh they're positively rude. More often than not, I'll just fry them in a little lemony butter, with a few threads of saffron, and eat with a large helping of delight. However, for something a little more involved, the following is delicious.

If you have planned sufficiently in advance to grow your own (about four days), or have access to a very good grocer/health food store, this looks gorgeous topped with a little micro-salad. That's sprouted seeds, to you and me. Try red radish and amaranth. You can buy both seeds and sprouters from good garden centres.

Serves two as a main course.
Halve the amount for a starter.

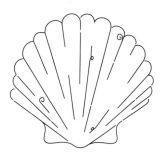

INGREDIENTS

- 1 butternut squash
- 1 tbsp melted butter
- 2 slices of prosciutto
- 150ml good chicken stock
- Olive oil
- 50g butter
- A dozen scallops
- A small truffle

(Sounds good already, hey?!)

Preheat the oven to 200C/390F. Cut the squash in half lengthways, and scoop out the seeds. Place on a baking dish and score deeply in a criss-cross pattern with a sharp knife. Brush with melted butter and place in the oven to bake for 30-40 minutes.

Meanwhile, brush a baking tray with olive oil and place the prosciutto on it. Bake in the top of the oven for 5 to 10 minutes, until crisp. Allow to cool on a wire rack.

When the squash is cooked and soft, remove from the oven. Scoop the flesh away from the skin. Using a handheld blender, blend 4 tbsp of the squash with 150ml of chicken stock, to form a smooth puree.

Before we cook the scallops, we need a bit of a chat. I can report that scallops, completely raw, are utterly delicious. Overcooked scallops, however, are a crime against the taste buds. I do think that if a scallop has been kind enough to sacrifice itself in order to feed us, we ought to do our best to serve it at its absolute best. So – this is my method. It may sound a little eccentric, but it works.

Heat the butter in a heavy based pan, over a medium-high heat. Calmly and without rushing, place the scallops in the pan, starting at 12 o'clock and working your way around. You will probably, if you have nice big scallops, have to spiral in towards the middle of the pan by the end. Count '5 elephants'. Starting back at 12 o'clock, turn the scallops over, calmly and without rushing. When you have turned them over, count a further '5 elephants'. Turn the pan off.

On a warmed plate, place a tablespoon of the squash puree. This may seem mean, but it is a good, rich, sweet flavour, and you don't want it to overpower the scallops. If you're feeling ambitious, go for a cheffy smear across the middle of the plate with the back of a spoon, but perhaps have a practice first – it's trickier than you'd think! Place the scallops on the plate, with a shaving of truffle under each scallop, allowing the truffle to infuse the scallop. Top with a prosciutto crisp and micro-salad, if you have it.

P.S. How to use the rest of your squash. Using the handheld blender while you've got it out, blend the rest of the squash with enough good stock (I would recommend chicken stock) to make a rich soup. Season with nutmeg and serve with a swirl of crème fraiche and, of course, a couple of truffle shavings!

Puddings

When Marion asked me to write the recipes for this book, I had not really thought of truffles as a sweet thing. After all, when it comes right down to it, they are a fungus – hard to imagine in a pudding.

However, knowing that in this case actions would most definitely speak louder than words, Marion gave me some truffled honey to taste. It was so good, it made my eyes pop. That got me thinking, and at one stage, much to my surprise, I found that more than half of the recipes I had thought up were for puddings!

The truffle lends itself so well to being used in recipes with cream and eggs – the starting point for so many puddings. And when it comes to chocolate – oof! Don't get me started.

So, preconceptions firmly aside, please, as you plunge into the glorious world of truffly puddings.

REAL Truffle Truffles

It just seemed obvious to me that someone should have made chocolate truffles using real truffles, and I figured there must be hundreds of recipes out there. But I looked and I hunted and I Googled, and no. There weren't.

I started thinking that, given the sheer amount of 'stuff' on the internet, the paucity of truffle truffle recipes was possibly due to it being a stupid idea, and put it out of my head. But it kept coming back and tapping me on the shoulder, so eventually it had to be tried.

I can't tell you how good these are. You'll just have to make some yourself. And I wholeheartedly advise you to put some of the ganache aside before adding the truffles so you can compare and contrast, because the difference is distinct, and the truffled version is sublime. 'Nuff said.

Makes: 30 – 40 truffles

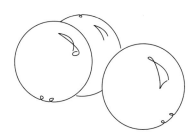

INGREDIENTS

- 225g plain chocolate
- 150ml full fat milk
- 75ml double cream
- 40g caster sugar
- 50g truffle

COATING OPTIONS:

- Raw cacao
- Gold leaf
- Edible glitter
- Icing sugar
- Chopped toasted hazelnuts
- Chocolate vermicelli...

REAL Truffle Truffles

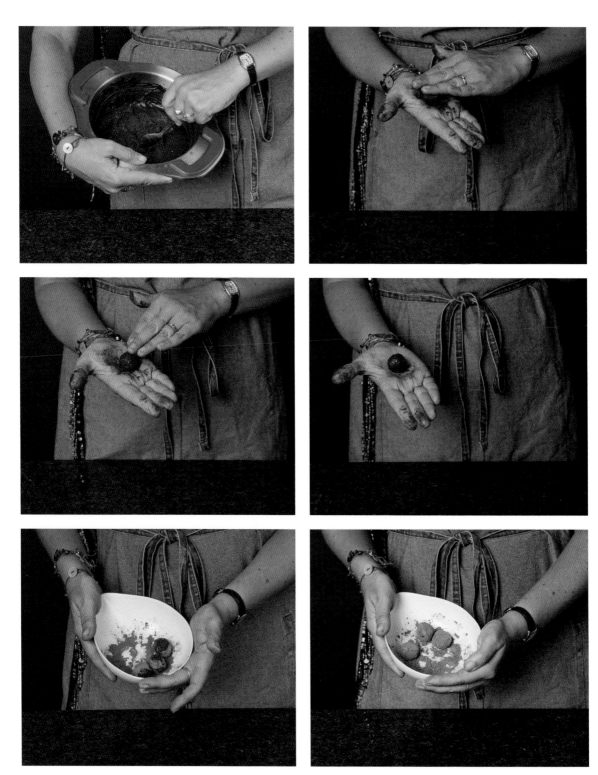

Break the chocolate into squares and melt in a *bain-marie*, or a bowl over a pan of hot water. Don't let the water boil, and don't let it touch the bottom of the bowl containing the chocolate.

Place the milk, double cream and caster sugar in a saucepan and bring barely to the boil. Remove from the heat and slowly add to the chocolate, stirring constantly. The mixture will temporarily look a bit scarily wrong – ignore this, it will all come back together!

Allow the ganache to cool to lukewarm, at which point it should be much thicker, but still more liquid than solid.

Peel the truffle (don't ditch the skins – add them to something else!) and chop it into tiny pieces. You can grate it, but I prefer the texture of little grains of truffle. I use a food chopper for this, as it quickly and effortlessly produces a very fine result.

Stir the truffle into the ganache, cover and place in the fridge until set.

Using a teaspoon or melon baller, carve out even amounts of truffled ganache and roll into balls. If you are going for serious presentation, you can weigh the ganache to make sure you get the same amount each time, but I quite enjoy picking a smaller or larger one according to how much I want to indulge myself!

Roll the balls very lightly in raw cacao powder, cocoa, chopped hazelnuts, edible gold leaf, glitter... you decide! I tend to stick to raw cacao powder (okay, with a bit of glitter dusted on – give 'em the old razzle-dazzle, darling!), as I love the fact that the only texture in these comes from the little chunks of truffle, but any of the other coatings would work, too.

If you are planning on giving some away, make sure you do this quickly, before you have chance to eat the lot. This is a serious warning. It happened to me, and I had some explaining to do...

– CHEF'S TIP –

If you pause before chilling, this sauce is outrageously good poured, still warm, over ice cream...

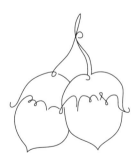

Thyme and
Truffle Ice Cream

I was on holiday with my husband in Lanzarote (where, by the way and much to our shamefully pre-conceived surprise, it is very easy to eat extremely well) when I first came across the notion of thyme ice-cream, which was served up with hot apple pie. I could hardly wait to get home to try figure out how to recreate the recipe. It worked. Here's a truffly version.

P.S. It is worth reviewing the custard recipe on P179 for tips on what to do if things go wrong at the custard stage!

Serves: 6

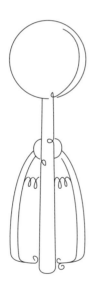

INGREDIENTS

- 1 pint full fat gold top Jersey milk

- ½ vanilla pod

- Bundle of fresh thyme

- Fresh truffles – approx 30g

- 6 egg yolks

- 125g caster sugar

- 150ml double cream

Pour the milk into a heavy saucepan. Slit the vanilla pod along its length and scrape the seeds out with the back of a knife. Add both to the milk, along with the bundle of thyme. If you absolutely want to avoid bits of thyme in the finished product, you can tie the thyme up in muslin for easy removal, but if you're not fussy, the thyme leaves do release an extra whoomph of flavour when bitten into.

Shave in some fresh truffle – as much as you like or have available. As a guide, six or seven shavings should do it, but feel free to add more if the urge strikes you. Heat the milk through slowly until almost boiling. Remove from the heat and cover, leaving to steep for half an hour. Whisk eggs and sugar together in a bowl. Remove vanilla pod and thyme and pour the cooled milk into the eggs and sugar, whisking while you pour.

Wash the pan up and return the mixture to it. Heat over a low to medium flame, stirring constantly for approximately 10 minutes, by which time the mixture should have visibly thickened. Allow the mixture to cool to room temperature, then place it in a covered bowl to chill in the fridge.

When you are ready to freeze it, whisk the cream until thickened and fold into the custard. If you have an ice-cream maker, pour the chilled creamy custard into it and switch on. When it seems to have got as thick as it's going to get (this will all depend on the type of ice-cream maker you have – you will know what it's doing and it's hard to go too wrong with one of these), transfer it into a container and place in the freezer.

If you have no ice-cream maker, pour the custard into a large plastic container and place in the freezer for an hour. Remove and beat it to within an inch of its life, either with a wooden spoon or an electric whisk. Repeat the freezing and beating twice more.

Before serving, move the ice cream to the fridge or a cool room for half an hour or so to allow it to soften and the flavours to emerge.

Serve with chocolate brownies – see recipe under Truffle Trifle – which magically magnify the truffle flavour. Also delicious with apple pie.

Truffled
Muscat Jelly

Delicate truffle flakes floating in a gently wobbling, barely set, golden wine jelly. So pretty. Serve sprinkled with pomegranate seeds or use to make Trufflebocker Glory. If you REALLY want to flash it up (literally), stir in some flakes of edible gold leaf at the same time as the grated truffle – ooh-la-la!

Serves: 6

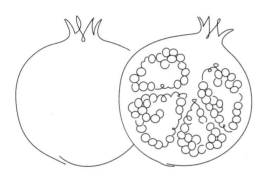

Peel your truffles. Add the peelings to your egg box, some rice or make butter with them – they are too good to throw away!

Pour the wine into a lidded jug or bowl (not metallic) and drop the peeled truffles in. Leave overnight.

Check your gelatine packet for quantities – a rule of thumb is that six leaves will set a pint and a half of liquid, but the leaves come in all different sizes, thicknesses and strengths, so beware, and proceed according to the specific instructions on YOUR pack of leaf gelatine! Place the appropriate amount of gelatine in a bowl with a little cold water and leave for 10 minutes.

Remove the truffles and pour the wine into a saucepan.

Warm through to just below boiling. Remove from heat. Scoop up the gelatine with your fingers and add to the wine. Whisk through to dissolve. Place saucepan in a sink of cold water to cool it down quickly. This is not essential, it just reduces the amount of time you need to wait before the next bit.

After 10-15 minutes, when the jelly is beginning to thicken a little, grate or shave the truffles into the mixture. If the slivers of truffle remain suspended, pour into wine glasses and refrigerate for several hours before serving. If not, just wait and stir occasionally, until the truffle doesn't sink to the bottom, then transfer to serving glasses and refrigerate for at least a couple of hours before serving.

INGREDIENTS

- 75cl Muscat
- Leaf gelatine – please see packet for quantity as all gelatine varies!
- Truffles – 10g
- 5 tbsp truffled sugar
- Edible gold leaf flakes (optional)
- Pomegranate seeds (optional)

Trufflebocker Glory

I grew up in Belgium, but holidays were spent with my grandparents in England. One set lived in Ramsgate, where we used to spend our summers pitch-and-putting along the cliffs of Thanet, and building endless sandy ships to sit in as the tide came in (don't try this at home etc., danger of drowning!). A huge treat was a visit to Morelli's Ice Cream Parlour for enormous Knickerbocker Glories, which my brother and I happily splashed and slurped our way through while our grandparents sipped milky coffee out of tall glasses set in (we thought) solid silver pierced holders. The height of sophistication! There were always dusty plaster of Paris models of the various ice cream options in the window, and glorious plastic statuettes of Botticelli's Venus, complete with fairy lights, miniature waterfalls and revolving fibre optics – sigh. It was perfect – kitsch heaven!

INGREDIENTS

– Meringues (home-made or shop-bought – but make them good ones! Remember that you'll have oodles of egg-whites left from making custard for the ice cream)

– One quantity of Thyme and Truffle Ice Cream (see recipe p169)

– One quantity of Truffled Muscat Jelly (see recipe p171)

– Vanilla syrup or Frangelico Hazelnut Liqueur

– Whipped cream

– Nuts, decorations, etc (see below)!

The quantities above are – hmm, shall we say a moveable feast? Bit of a tricky one to call! Do you fancy a pint glass full or a thimble – or somewhere in between? So – I've told you WHAT you'll need. When it comes to how much of it – well, it is entirely a matter for you!

Take a look at your receptacles, measure the anticipated enthusiasm of your fellow diners, and build them a pudding to remember!

As you can only really put this together at the last minute anyway, you can alter the amounts to fit the appetites. You could even put all the ingredients on the table, with a variety of glasses (and, of course, decorations ranging from the Delia to the Del Boy) and invite your guests to build their own.

Pour a little syrup or Frangelico into the bottom of a Knickerbocker Glory glass, should you have such a delightfully decadent thing in your possession. If not, use a sundae glass. If no sundae glass, I think these look very pretty (and are far more delicate if not so wantonly indulgent) served in champagne glasses.

Add a little jelly followed by a scoop of ice cream. Break a little (but not toooo little) meringue into the glass, and spoon over a little whipped cream. Repeat. Obviously you must use your own judgement when determining the quantities of each ingredient, depending on the size of your glass and how many layers you want to build up.

When the glass is full, drizzle the final result with syrup or Frangelico.

I don't want to spoil your fun, here, so if you want to keep it classy, maybe just sprinkle a few toasted chopped hazelnuts on the top, or some nibbed pistachios. Truffles and hazelnuts are immensely complementary flavours, each bringing out something truly special in the other.

Meanwhile, back to your magnificent Trufflebocker Glory! If you want to go the whole hog, please feel free to go berserk with squirty cream, Smarties and hundreds and thousands, even a maraschino cherry on the top. Ooh, and a paper parasol! Whatever floats your boat. This pudding really ought to make you feel fabulously and childishly happy, so do whatever it takes!

Truffled Rice Pudding

Luxurious comfort food – rice pud fit for a king! If you have time, leave a truffle in with your rice overnight – as it does with the eggs, so will it impart its flavour to the rice. Such a generous ingredient, it is! When you pour the truffly milk over the rice, try to make sure that you poke the truffle shavings down a little – you don't want them floating right on the surface or they will dry out and the flavour will be impaired.

Serves: 6

Preheat the oven to 160C/320F.

Lightly butter a stoneware dish. Add the uncooked rice.

Warm the milk through and stir in the sugar and truffle shavings, together with a grate of nutmeg.

Pour over the rice and place in the oven for 45 minutes.

Serve with rosehip or other hedgerow jelly.

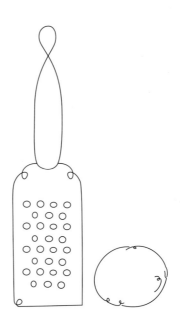

INGREDIENTS

- A little butter
- 80g pudding rice
- 1 pint gold top milk
- 1 truffle
- 1tbsp sugar
- Nutmeg

Bread and Butter Pudding

I realise that it's really not done to big up your own recipes, but unfortunately, in this case, I just can't help it. This is so tasty that I could eat the whole lot myself, in a little tent in a dark and secret corner. I usually use panettone to make Bread and Butter Pudding, but in this case it overpowers the truffles, so best not.

Serves: 6

Place butter, extra thick cream, sugar and truffle in a small blender or food processor and process until fairly smooth – but let's not worry toooo much, shall we? Spread the bread with the truffle butter mixture and arrange, butter side up, in an ovenproof dish, approx 28-30cm in diameter.

Warm the milk and cream in a pan, but do not bring to the boil.

Whisk together the eggs and sugar and pour into the warm milk, whisking throughout.

Pour the custard gently around the bread into the dish, so that the bread is not saturated in custard, and it doesn't melt all the butter off. It will soak the custard up nicely from underneath.

Allow to stand for at least half an hour while you preheat the oven to 160C/320F.

Sprinkle extra sugar over and place in the oven for 30 minutes.

INGREDIENTS

– 50g butter

– 60ml extra thick double cream

– 1tbsp sugar

– 1 truffle, peeled

– 5 to 10 slices of white bread or English muffins, thinly sliced and cut into triangles*

  * Quantity here will depend on your pattern and how much overlap you like - very flexible...

FOR THE CUSTARD:

– 350ml gold top milk

– 50ml double cream

– 2 eggs (truffled, if you have had time!)

– 20g sugar plus a little extra for sprinkling

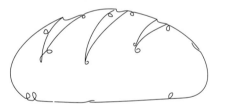

Truffled Custard

This is a good starting point for many recipes. Eggs. Full fat milk. Vanilla. Truffles. Can't go wrong, really...

Makes: A pint and a half of custard

Pour the milk into a heavy saucepan. Slit the vanilla pod along its length and scrape the seeds out with the back of a knife. Add both to the milk and shave in some fresh truffle – be generous.

Heat the milk through slowly until almost boiling. Remove from the heat and cover, leaving to steep for half an hour. Try to resist the urge to keep going over and smelling it! Actually, don't – it's a great pleasure.

Whisk eggs and sugar together in a bowl. Remove vanilla pod and pour the cooled milk into the eggs and sugar, whisking while you pour.

Return the mixture to the (clean) pan and heat over a low to medium flame, stirring all the time. After about 10 minutes, the mixture should have visibly thickened. This may take a little longer than you expect, but try to take it any quicker and you will end up with sweet scrambled eggs.

If by any chance the mixture does start to curdle, you can save it if you're quick. Have a sink half full of cold water standing by, so that if the eggs begin to set you can sink the saucepan into it and whisk the contents like fury to cool it down. Then cautiously return to the heat and carry on. If you proceed throughout with patience, however, you will not need to do this!

This recipe will produce a custard with the consistency of double cream. If you need a thicker custard – a *crème patissiere* – add 1 1/2 tbsp of cornflour to the eggs and sugar before whisking.

Voila, truffled custard! Now a host of desserts are ready to enter your world... truffled custard tarts, or profiteroles... Mmmm!

INGREDIENTS

- 1 pint full fat Jersey milk – real gold top stuff
- ½ vanilla pod
- Fresh truffles – approx. 20g, but as always this is to taste
- 5 egg yolks
- 80g caster sugar

Chocolate Brownies

There is no truffle content to this recipe, but you need brownies for the trifle, and you may as well make them delicious! These are also fabulous with the truffle ice cream.

Serves: 6 – 12

Line a 23cm square baking tray with greaseproof paper.

Melt butter and chocolate together over a very slow heat in a large, heavy based saucepan or *bain-marie*, if you would like to be on the safe side. Don't rush this – if you overheat the chocolate it will separate, and you will have to ditch it and start all over again.

Meanwhile, beat together eggs, sugar and vanilla.

When the chocolate mixture has melted, allow it to cool slightly, then beat in the egg and sugar mixture in the saucepan. Add the flour and beat to combine.

Pour the batter into the prepared baking tray and bake for approximately 25 minutes, in the centre of the oven.

The middle of these brownies should be almost fudge-like in texture. You may feel they are not sufficiently cooked for your liking. If so, I give you my blessing to cook them for longer. For me, it's precisely the dense, melting, fudginess of them which I find irresistible. And remember that they will continue to cook as they cool.

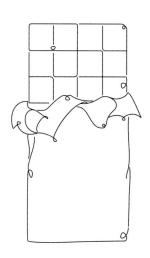

INGREDIENTS

- 250g butter at room temperature
- 250g dark chocolate – the darker the better
- 4 eggs
- 10ml good vanilla extract – not essence!
- 330g caster sugar
- 150g plain flour (I use Dove's Farm wheat-free flour and it works brilliantly)

Truffle Trifle

I freely admit that I thought up this recipe purely on the basis that I liked its name. I toyed with it and rejected it many times, as I couldn't see how fruit and spongy jelly (or jellified sponge) would go with truffle. I considered using the Truffled Muscat Jelly recipe, but it just didn't grab me. Still, the name kept popping back into my mind. One morning, I woke up with the recipe complete in my brain. Wonderful thing, the subconscious! Unlike Samuel Taylor Coleridge, I was not interrupted by a Person from Porlock, and managed to get it down on paper before I forgot it. What really did it was the whole truffle/hazelnut complementary flavour thing (see recipe for Trufflebocker Glory). Once I was thinking hazelnuts rather than flaked almonds and Frangelico (which is a hazelnut liqueur – aha, you see where this is going...?!) rather than sherry, the rest was easy. And blooming tasty!.

Serves: 6

Cut the brownies into 3cm cubes. Place them in the trifle bowl and add half of the Frangelico. Allow this to soak in for 15 minutes, then add the rest. Feel free to add more. If you want to make it a non-alcoholic pudding, you could add a hazelnut syrup such as Monin syrup for coffee. Beware, though – it's sweet stuff, so you'll have to tread a fine line between 'enough hazelnut' and 'too sweet'. Safer to stick to the booze?

Sprinkle the raspberries and 125g of the hazelnuts over the brownies, and pour over the custard. Place in the fridge and allow the custard to set slightly.

Whip the cream to soft peaks and spoon it over the custard. Sprinkle on the reserved hazelnuts.

Eat.

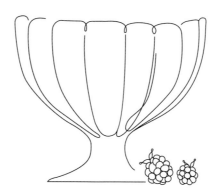

INGREDIENTS

- ½ quantity Chocolate Brownies – see recipe above
- Half a cup of Frangelico
- 250g raspberries
- 150g chopped roasted hazelnuts
- 500ml truffled custard (with a teaspoon of cornflour added) (see recipe p179)
- 500ml whipping cream

Truffled Honey Cakes with Champagne Syllabub

Sublime little cakes with that so very British thing – a syllabub. I used to think that syllabub sounded frightfully complicated to make, but it is so very easy! This pudding packs a good flavour punch, so you don't need a lot. While it may not look like a slimming pudding (butter, sugar, double cream... not your typical diet ingredients!), I am a big believer in indulging yourself with a little of what you fancy. This one ticks those boxes!

Makes 30 petit-four sized cakes, but I expect you won't mind having some left over... Syllabub serves: 6

INGREDIENTS

– For the cakes (makes 30 small cakes):

– 250g butter at room temperature

– 250g light soft brown sugar

– 3 eggs

– 250g Wessex Mill gluten-free bread flour

– 2 tsp baking powder

– 5 tbsp milk

– 3 tsp truffled honey

GLAZE:

– 50g butter

– 50g honey

SYLLABUB:

– 300ml double cream

– 50ml Champagne or good sparkling wine

– 1 tbsp icing sugar

– 4 tbsp lemon curd

CAKES:

Preheat oven to 170C/340F.

Grease and flour a mini-muffin pan. If you don't have a non-stick pan, you will have to line it with petit fours cases. This works fine, but gives a slightly less sophisticated finish.

Combine all ingredients and beat until smooth. You can do this in a bowl with a wooden spoon, or in a food processor. The decision here is purely based on which you'd rather wash up afterwards.

Transfer to pan and bake for 15 minutes, checking regularly towards the end, as ovens vary enormously.

Melt butter in heavy-based pan. Add honey and simmer over a low heat, stirring until sugar is dissolved.

Remove cakes from oven, turn out and allow to cool. Brush with warm glaze, and serve with...

SYLLABUB:

Whip the cream with the sugar until it reaches soft peaks.

Fold in the Champagne and swirl through the lemon curd.

Serve in a little liqueur glass with a couple of cakes.

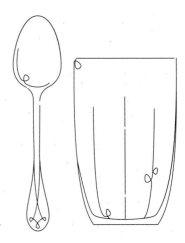

Truffleccino

Hot, truffly, frothy, alcoholic – you can't beat it after a brisk walk on a cold day, in place of an Irish coffee, as a welcoming first drink for a Boxing Day drinks party, or – well, find your own excuses!

Again, those complementary hazelnut/truffle flavours...

Serves: 2

In a heavy pan, bring milk to just below the boil, then turn the heat down to low while you shave in the truffles.

Cover and remove from the heat, allowing to steep for at least half an hour, preferably longer.

Return to a low heat and warm through to drinking temperature. Add cacao powder, Frangelico, and vanilla syrup to taste. Exercise restraint with the syrup, as it sweetens up very quickly. Obviously, exercise no such thing with the Frangelico!

There are a number of different ways to make what is essentially hot milk into frothy hot milk. There's whisking like fury, or using a special milk whisk. You can use one of those lovely glass jugs with the plunger inside and plunge it up and down until the required frothiness is achieved. Or you could use a proprietary electrical frother of the type which comes with certain makes of coffee machine (*coughs Aeroccino*). In any case, whatever method you choose, froth the milk up and serve in shot glasses, garnished with toasted chopped hazelnuts and raw cacao. Then sit back and sip, bathed in the glow of a drink well made (extra Frangelico helps with the whole 'glow' thing...).

INGREDIENTS

- ½ pint full fat milk
- ½ truffle
- ½ tsp raw cacao powder
- 1 tbsp Frangelico hazelnut liqueur
- Vanilla syrup
- Toasted chopped hazelnuts to garnish

Treasury of Truffliness

While working on the book, my mind was inevitably filled with things to do with truffles. Kind of the whole point, right?

Equally inevitably, not all of these ideas fitted into the headings of starters, main courses, puddings etc...

I therefore started a little file entitled Miscellany.

When it came down to writing a chapter heading, however, Marion D felt that 'Miscellany' was a rather insulting title for a collection of wonderful – er – miscellaneous (!) uses for truffles, so we dug around for another title. Cornucopia seemed too grand and twee, all at once, as did many other options which are best consigned to the 'Let's not and say we did' bin.

So a Treasury of Truffliness it is.

Oh! Before I forget... At a casual glance, this chapter may appear to be 'Methods of making your truffles last for a long time'. Do not be fooled. While the butter, if frozen in portions, is a satisfactory way of preserving a glut of truffles (should you be so lucky to be blessed with such a thing), the other recipes are not designed for this purpose.

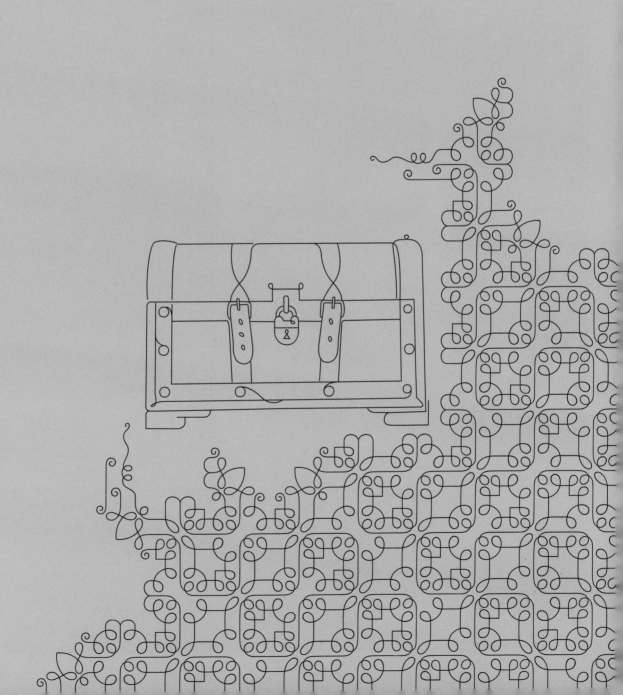

Truffle Butter

Difficult though it may be to believe, if you're lucky enough to be the owner of an exceptional truffle hound, and have the further good fortune to find a good location, you may well find yourself with a surfeit of truffles! Although they will keep for up to a week in normal conditions, the flavour will diminish over time. A useful thing to do with them is to make truffle butter.

I use salted butter, but you can use either.

Weigh your truffle and use ten times the weight of butter to truffle. Place butter in a bowl big enough to allow mixing space. Using a medium grade Microplane ® grater, grate the whole truffle, including the skin, directly on to the butter. There is a great deal of flavour in the skins, and it is a shame, in my opinion, to waste them. However, if you are worried about the occasional graininess affecting the texture and wish to peel them, please don't let me stand in your way.

Mash the butter and truffle together with a fork.

Place a square of cling film on a cold surface and roll the truffle butter into a cylinder. Keep any truffle butter that you need for immediate use in the fridge. For the rest, divide into portions in an ice cube tray, freeze and transfer to freezer bags. Store in the freezer and remove to use as and when it is required.

SUGGESTED USES FOR TRUFFLE BUTTER:

On toast or crumpets, just plain delicious;
Stuffed into chicken breasts, à la Kiev;
Dotted on steak;
Roughly crushed into new potatoes;
Melted onto popcorn;
Stuffed under the skin on the breasts of pheasants or partridges, then roasted;
Melted into mashed potato – divine...
Über-posh jacket potatoes.

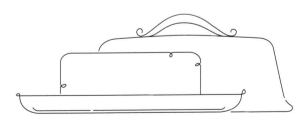

INGREDIENTS

- 5g truffles per 50g butter
  at room temperature

Truffled Mayonnaise

If you've never made mayonnaise before, please do not be put off. It is really very easy indeed, and, possibly more importantly, very quick.

This recipe makes approximately 175ml of finished mayonnaise. This is the smallest amount you can make, unless you want to start dividing egg yolks in half. If you need more, by all means multiply the amount, but please ensure that you use it within a day – this is the shelf life for truffles in this form.

As I wanted the truffle to shine through as the dominant flavour, I have deliberately made the mayonnaise itself quite bland. You will find, if you use olive oil in a mayonnaise, the finished product can often leave you with a slightly bitter aftertaste. Some very mild, light olive oils work well, but I have used sunflower oil here, as it works every time. I'd hate you to end up with bitter mayonnaise!

INGREDIENTS

- 1 egg yolk
- 1 tsp mild mustard – tarragon mustard if you can get it
- 150ml sunflower oil
- A drop of truffle oil (optional)
- Juice of half a lemon
- 20g truffle

Mince the truffle very finely. Measure the oil into a jug which pours nicely, and have the lemon juice standing ready. In a largish bowl, whisk the egg yolk and the mustard together. You can do this by hand if it makes you feel good, but using an electric whisk is equally acceptable. And very easy.

Add a small amount of the oil and whisk in. Then, in a slow but steady stream, add the rest of the oil, whisking continuously. I find this process, the lightening of the colour and the increase in the opacity, magical to watch, every time.

When all the oil has been added, slowly add the lemon juice, still whisking.

Have a look at the texture, and decide whether you're happy with it. I like quite a light mayonnaise, both in consistency and colour, so at this point I would tend to whisk in a little ice cold water, but this is personal preference.

Once you are happy with the mayonnaise, stir in the truffle. It is best, if you can, not to settle down at this point with the bowl, the spoon and a bib, although I approve of the impulse to do so. Instead, leave the mayonnaise in the fridge for at least an hour to allow the truffle flavour to permeate nicely.

This mayonnaise works beautifully in a number of dishes. Elsewhere in the book, you will find recipes for Barbecued Asparagus with Truffle Mayonnaise (p111), Hard-boiled Eggs with Truffled Mayonnaise (p115), and Truffled Potato Salad (up next).

– CHEF'S TIP... –

I have never had a problem making mayonnaise from scratch (just to reiterate the first sentence in this recipe – it's EASY), but disasters do happen at the most unexpected times. So. Have a spare egg ready, and a spare bowl. This should be at room temperature, but I'm assuming you don't keep your eggs in the fridge (if you do – don't! If supermarkets, who naturally want to give things as long a shelf life as possible, don't put their eggs in the fridge, you can trust that you really, really do not need to do so!). If your mayo splits, separate the egg, and whisk the yolk, in the spare bowl, with a little tepid water until it just begins to thicken. Then slowly, slowly add the mayonnaise, whisking constantly.

Truffled Mayonnaise
and Potato Salad

Make more than you think you'll need. It's nice...

Scrub the potatoes, leaving their skins as intact as possible. If you have very small new potatoes, you can leave them whole, but if not, cut into pieces.

Place them in a pan with plenty of cold water, and bring to the boil. Simmer for approximately 15-20 minutes, depending on the size of the potatoes. To check if they are done, pierce a potato with a sharp (non-serrated) knife. If the potato falls off when the knife is held vertically (with the potato pointing down), they're done.

Pour potatoes and water into a sieve or colander, and refresh with cold water.

Put the potatoes aside to cool thoroughly before mixing with the mayonnaise. Again, mixing together when warm will result in the mayonnaise looking oily, and as if the potato salad has sat in the sun for a couple of hours. Not nice.

Add some freshly chopped chives, a pinch of good salt and a grind of black pepper. Stir until all is evenly coated.

Sprinkle with chive flowers, if you have them, or extra chopped chives if not.

INGREDIENTS

- Generous handful of new potatoes per person
- Tablespoon of truffled mayonnaise per person
- Chives
- Seasoning
- Chive flowers, if available

Truffled
Vinaigrettes

I have experimented with various truffled vinaigrettes, but have failed to come up with a single vinaigrette which everyone can agree on as being the best. People seem to have fallen into two distinct camps, with pretty much exactly half of them preferring each of the two following vinaigrettes. It seems to be purely a matter of personal taste, so you must decide for yourself, I'm afraid!

The quantities given below make a small amount of vinaigrette, as this is strictly a make-and-use recipe (see notes re truffle oil on p76). There is, of course, nothing to stop you from making a far larger batch in advance, leaving out the truffle. You can then simply decant a small amount at a time and add the truffle an hour or so in advance of use, to give it time to infuse.

MUSTARD VINAIGRETTE:

Place all ingredients in a small jar and shake.

SHERRY VINAIGRETTE:

Whisk the first four ingredients together with the seasoning. Add the oil in a steady stream, whisking continuously.

Both vinaigrettes work well dressing a salad of mixed leaves served with grilled chicken or panfried pigeon breast – that woodland connection again. Add some chopped roasted hazelnuts to the dish for extra crunch and yet another layer of flavour. Also works very well as a dressing for warm asparagus

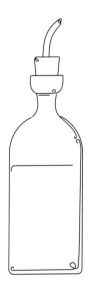

MUSTARD VINAIGRETTE:

- 2 tbsp olive oil

- 2 tbsp white wine vinegar

- 1 tsp tarragon mustard

- 1 tsp finely minced truffle

SHERRY VINAIGRETTE:

- 1½ tbsp sherry vinegar – try to find
  an aged one as younger ones can be
  quite sharp

- 1½ tsp lemon juice

- 1 tsp sweet sherry

- 15g finely minced truffle

- Salt & pepper

- 4½ tbsp rapeseed oil

Truffle Potato Chutney

I wanted to make a truffle chutney, but was having difficulty envisaging how it would work in a normal chutney background. I felt it would have to fight to make itself noticed amongst all that vinegar and fruit. I decided that the preserving elements of the chutney were not what I was looking for, which cut out the need for either an excess of oil, vinegar or sugar. Good start!

I'm a keen Indian cook, and it struck me that in Indian cuisine, chutney simply seems to mean condiment. It can be a fresh or a preserved condiment, and does not have to resemble in any way what we think of as an English chutney – which, by the way, I am equally fond of – but I digress...

Back to truffles! Extensive research and experimentation produced the following chutney. Please remember: this is a condiment – it is NOT a method of preserving truffles, so do not try to keep it for more than a day in the fridge. In my house we're lucky if we've got any left after just a few hours.

Scrub the potatoes and cut into 1cm dice. Do not peel potatoes.

Place the potatoes and sugar in a pan and cover with cold water. Bring to the boil and simmer until cooked through. Drain and set aside.

Sauté the shallots in the butter until soft. Add the cider and reduce, over a low to medium heat, until you are left with no liquid in the pan, stirring constantly.

Add the shallots, hazelnuts and truffle to the potatoes, and stir in gently.

Serve with cold meats, fresh warm bread and green salad.

See recipe on p133 for Truffled Potato Chutney Cakes with Poached Eggs

INGREDIENTS

- 350g potatoes
- 25g sugar
- 1 banana shallot, or three small shallots
- Knob of butter
- 100ml dry cider
- 20g hazelnuts
- 25g finely sliced truffle

Other uses for Truffled Mayonnaise

The world is really your oyster, with this, so please feel free to experiment (and let me know if you come up with something fabulous!).

However, just to get you started, here are some ideas:

There are few sandwiches which are not improved by a good dollop of this mayonnaise. Egg mayonnaise is an obvious contender for 'Best Sandwich' title. However, ham, watercress and truffled mayo is also delicious. Chicken, lettuce and truffled mayo, with a little extra salt on the lettuce is divine. And if you want to keep it simple, a plain green salad and mayo sandwich is hard to beat.

Mix with vinaigrette if you like a creamy salad dressing.

Delicious with cold smoked meats.

Serve with poached salmon for an easy, impressive buffet dish.

Finally, as someone who grew up in Belgium, how could I not recommend this with a nice big portion of chips, and perhaps a decent sized helping of moules. And an ice cold Belgian beer... Now we're talking...!

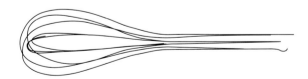

Equipment and Stockists

While specialist tools are not indispensable for dealing with truffles, the following are helpful.

For shaving truffles into slivers, a mandoline or specialist truffle shaver is useful but can be tricky to operate if you are not accustomed to using one. If you would like to preserve your knuckles and fingernails, I therefore recommend a garlic slicer. I use the one produced by Pampered Chef, as it is easy to operate and wash. It will allow you to produce perfect, regular slivers of truffle simply by twisting. Brilliant.

For chopping the truffles into teeny tiny pieces, for Truffle Truffles, I use a food chopper. Again, the Pampered Chef version is the best I have found – it is robust, sharp, has a higher return (meaning it does not jam easily and you can fit larger food items under it), and comes with a 10-year guarantee.

As mentioned throughout the book, Microplane ® graters are by far the best way to grate truffles, producing clean shards rather than bruised lumps. These are widely available from various producers – just look for the Microplane ® trademark.

All three of the above are available directly from Maz via maz.pennington@gmail.com.

Dove's Farm – flour
Truffle Cheese – www.vickiescheese.com
Truffles – www.trufflehuntersdogschool.com
Raw cacao powder – www.chocchick.com
Giant Wild Rice – Tilda rice – www.tilda.com

PART FOUR: SOURCING YOUR TRUFFLE

To Forage or
Not To Forage?

If you want to cook a recipe with truffles in – you need a truffle. Where do you get one from? Now that you are positively certain that they do in fact grow happily in Britain, the most romantic notion of all is to walk through a dreamy woodland with your dog telling you where they all are. Yes, that is quite possible if you have a trained dog and own the woodland in question. If you cannot satisfy both of these requirements, the next best scenario is to have a trained dog and permission from the owner of the woodland to search for truffles.

You most probably still feel that a truffle is the ultimate foraging goal, not at least because of unrealistically high price tags that most people associate with them. I hate to be a spoilsport but there is bad news here if you had just thought you were on to the latest get-rich-quick scheme. The huge, huge, huge truffle prices that hit the headlines tend to be for the Italian White Truffles (*Tuber magnatum*). Our indigenous black Summer Truffles (*Tuber aestivum*), are far more modestly priced. That is more work if you are selling but good news if you are buying. The situation is still not so straightforward, read on.

Foraging is now almost a buzz word in magazines and television programmes. I'm all for it. There is nothing better than being able to walk along and identify a wild strawberry. Sorry I lied, yes there is, walking along, identifying and eating a wild strawberry is much better, even if the strawberry in question is barely larger than a pea. Mufti likes them too. Blackberries I adore, and could probably happily survive on crumbles and jam if anything nasty happened to the rest of the world.

Unfortunately there are very few plants growing wild that I can identify safely enough to eat, and believe it or not, I simply don't do mushrooms. I know lots of people who do and I admire their skills and knowledge. Some of the mushrooms, which don't kill you, are able to command high prices in the marketplace. This in itself can create a problem because many people simply do not realise that in this country you are not allowed to sell food that has been foraged. In simple terms, you may forage for your own meals, but that's all.

This information is enough to flabbergast many people. The thought that you are not allowed to sell a few posh mushrooms to your nearest gastro pub might seem outrageous. Don't shoot the messenger, I didn't write the laws, but actually as I am now heavily involved with both harvesting, and hopefully producing truffles I realise how these rules and regs have come about.

Truffles admittedly are harder to find than mushrooms, but in terms of value, have even better credentials. Please check the restrictions on foraging before setting off on a mission.

It does not matter where you are, reckless or over-enthusiastic digging (from either man or dog) can do much damage to the underground truffle mycorrhizal growth. It can take many years for this to form and so truffles should be collected with the minimum disturbance to the surrounding area. My customers always laugh when I produce my truffle hunting equipment. One well-mannered dog, trained not to dig, and a cake fork, about four inches long and rather blunt.

Of course I do go out looking for new truffle sites; the thrill of the chase is still with me after all these years. I know truffles can't run away but finding one is still so very, very exciting. I adore walking along a country road and finding a truffle in the hedgerow. Even this is technically out of bounds. I would never recommend eating a truffle from the roadside because of the amount of cars on our roads these days, and more often than not, I can leave the truffle behind to allow for the natural spread of truffle spores. What it does do is to help me chart the spread of truffles and identify any nearby woodlands that could be good potential private sites. Landowners without exception have always greeted me warmly!

Not many readers will however be able to consider foraging for truffles. To go looking without a dog is real 'needle in a haystack' situation and I think you are more likely to grow old before finding a truffle on your own. That brings us round to the most likely scenario of having to buy your truffles. Your choices are fresh, frozen or processed.

Advice for Buying

In my opinion, there is only one way you should consider buying truffles, and that is fresh. I would suggest to you that the little processed ones you might find in jars are best avoided.

There are two huge price drivers with truffles. The first is availability and the second is freshness. Truffles are, like any other harvest, entirely dependent on good growing conditions (yes, even underground) and, unfortunately, they have a very short shelf life – perhaps seven to ten days. Time is of the essence.

Another point to remember is that truffles are seasonal; therefore your choice will vary according to the time of year.

Your most likely source of truffles is from the internet. There are hundreds of adverts for them, and let's remember you are entering a global market place. Beware, don't happen across a picture and think the truffle must be the right kind if it looks like one of the pictures in this book. Several different kinds of truffle have the same, or a very similar outward appearance. Your best protection comes from using the Latin names for the specific type of truffle you want (see page 221) AND only to buy from a reputable source. You really must check that you are getting exactly what you have paid for.

It is rather an irony that one of the major attributes of the truffle, its ability to impart its flavour to all that surrounds it, can also be used adversely in unscrupulous situations. Inferior truffles can be stored, even briefly, with luxurious ones to have their aroma enhanced. Unfortunately this practice would not be enough to lift the flavour of a poor truffle above the level of disappointing. It cannot come as a surprise to you that exploitation in the world of truffles still exists today, but at least now you are forewarned.

I do hope you will already have noticed that I take great pride in the quality of the British black Summer Truffle. I would hate you to be disappointed with your first taste, when really it should result in what Maz would describe as an 'eye-crossing, jaw dropping WOW!' Even the poached egg recipe will do this for you!

A fresh truffle in good condition is firm to the touch and the aroma should be beautiful. Any softness might indicate that there is internal damage or aging. If your truffle is totally soft, it is either exceedingly elderly or has come out of the freezer. Some maintain that truffles can be frozen. Yes, they physically can, but their qualities change and so they must be handled differently. For example, all the internal marbling would be lost, so this would spoil the appearance of your truffle shavings. Besides which, in this instance, I would not class a frozen truffle as a fresh truffle. If your truffle has a weak aroma, it is probably under-ripe. It may improve a little by waiting a day or two but you won't get a dramatic change as you would, for example, with a banana. All these factors should be reflected in the price.

Some people might still not know what to expect with reference to the quality of what they are buying. Truffles can be all sorts of funny shapes and sizes. The shape of your truffle really doesn't matter unless you want uniformly shaped shavings, otherwise don't worry about it. We do not currently have an established grading system for truffles here as exists on mainland Europe, which is why I recommended earlier that you must establish that you are buying from a reputable source. Typically in France or Italy a Grade One truffle would be whole (no pieces chopped off), the peridium would be virtually undamaged, a minute amount of scuffing where truffles had knocked together I think is acceptable. You might see a deliberate tiny slice missing. This is not damage, it is where someone has checked the truffle for ripeness by revealing a little of the inner gleba colouring. Blatant damage should not be there. Very often truffles are damaged as they are removed from the ground but this should be reflected in their price and they should not be classified as top grade. Don't get too hung up about it though, the real value for your money is in the ripeness, and that automatically includes the colouring and flavour.

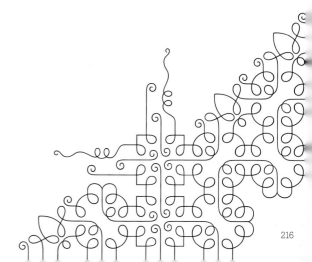

Study the photograph which I have compiled especially for this section. The top two truffles ought to please anyone. The truffle with a large area of missing peridium looks as though it has been nibbled and this would disappoint me if I had requested a top grade one. The last truffle would also disappoint me, not because a tiny sliver had been removed, but because the pale colour reveals it clearly is not ripe.

Many vendors now sell truffle pieces, as indeed I do. I think this is a really good idea – a little truffle can go a long way. What may surprise and I hope, please you is that a very nice piece of black Summer Truffle might only cost a few pounds, so you don't have to win the lottery to try one.

Good

Good

Nibbled

Unripe

218

Purchasing Power

Truffles are sold by weight, usually grams, and can be sold whole or in pieces. Whichever you decide on it is always best to compare a few prices, I have seen some astronomical figures quoted and I cannot think of any situation where these could be justified. To help you tune in, truffles costing 20p a gram would be £200 a kilogram; 35p a gram would be £350 a kilogram; and so on. Always do the gram to kilogram conversion, even if we are talking 'black diamonds', let's keep our feet firmly on the ground!

I cannot advise you on how much truffle to buy for your individual needs but do not worry about wasting any (ridiculous thought!). Even the tiniest leftover scrap could be used to make truffle butter to name but one idea. I decided to include my shavings demo photograph. If you are making a dish with truffle shavings, just look at how many you can make with 20g of truffle.

Choose the Right Truffle

<u>TRUFFLES USED IN OUR RECIPES</u>

As I mentioned earlier, each truffle has a different taste and different cooking attributes. They are not always interchangeable in recipes; therefore it is best to make sure you buy the right kind.

<u>BLACK SUMMER TRUFFLE, *TUBER AESTIVUM*</u>
(You may also see Tuber aestivum/ uncinatum,
or Tuber aestivum = Tuber uncinatum.)

These truffles are probably the most versatile of all for culinary purposes, but are not so strongly flavoured or as aromatic as the more expensive French or Italian truffles. They grow widespread throughout Europe; therefore please note that those advertised for sale in Britain may not have grown in Britain. Prices will be at their most affordable in the early summer when the new season is just getting underway and then will rise steadily towards Christmas and even beyond if growing conditions permit. A few pounds (well, under £20) could get you started.

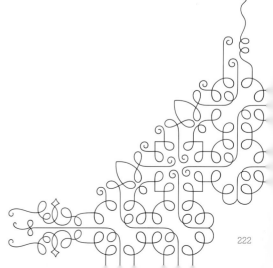

BURGUNDY TRUFFLE, *TUBER UNCINATUM*

*(You may also see Tuber uncinatum/aestivum,
or Tuber uncinatum = Tuber aestivum.)*

The Burgundy Truffle has, as you will probably have guessed,
been attributed with the area name in France with which it is
famously associated. It was formerly thought that the Summer
Truffle and the Burgundy Truffle were different species, but now
the scientists have been able to ascertain that these are indeed
one in the same, hence the rather laborious Latin terminology.
Despite this, they are often still referred to separately.
The 'Burgundy' Truffle is harvested in the autumn. I am sure
this is a situation where it would be useful if we could adopt
a 'variety' name after the genus and species; it would be absurd
to suggest that regional differences do not exist.

Other Popular Truffles

PÉRIGORD TRUFFLE, *TUBER MELANOSPORUM*

Again, this truffle has taken on the French area name, which made it famous and is often referred to by this alone. It does grow in other countries too but I cannot blame the French for wanting the title to this magnificent truffle! Altogether more powerful than the black Summer Truffle, it is harvested during the winter months and also referred to as the black Winter Truffle. When this truffle is unavailable (or you have seen a gorgeous sounding recipe and want to have a more economical test run) the black Summer Truffle can be substituted – remembering the flavour will not be so strong.

If you were just to take a quick glance at the picture of this truffle you could easily mistake it for a black Summer Truffle and buy one in error. The differences in taste and price are greater than the differences in the peridium and inner colouring. This illustrates my point about needing to check the Latin names when ordering.

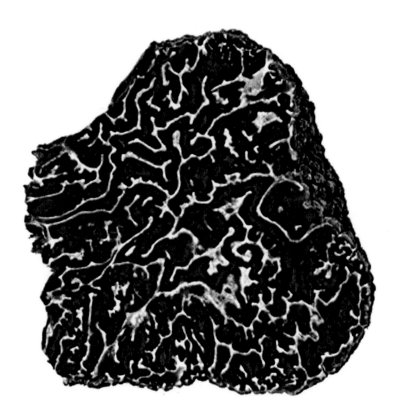

When fully ripe the inner gleba becomes an inky black colour.

This photograph has been reproduced by the kind permission of Ian Hall.

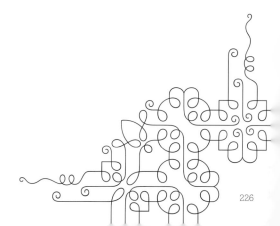

ANOTHER BLACK WINTER TRUFFLE, *TUBER BRUMALE*

You might have noticed in my earlier words that I can hardly give this truffle the time of day. This is purely my own opinion; apparently lots of other people do like them! To elaborate, I find the aroma is rather unpleasant and overpowering. *Tuber brumale* is often processed (to make it more palatable) and sold in little bottles in delicatessens.

I have included *Tuber brumale* here for a very good reason. Please read the next paragraph then compare it to the one above in italics.

If you were just to take a quick glance at the picture of this truffle you could easily mistake it for a black Summer Truffle or a Périgord Truffle and buy one in error. The differences in taste and price are greater than the differences in the peridium and inner colouring. This illustrates my point about needing to check the Latin names when ordering.

Typically the peridium (outer covering) of this truffle is very easy to scratch off and the white veins inside are much broader than in other truffles.

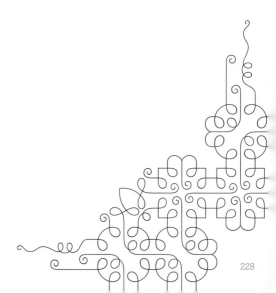

THE ITALIAN WHITE TRUFFLE, *TUBER MAGNATUM*

Also known as the Piedmont Truffle, geography and national pride to the fore again! Unlike the others, this white truffle (there are other smaller, lower ranking, white truffles, e.g. *Tuber borchii*) is almost exclusive to Italy. Highly prized and highly priced, this truffle is best uncooked, served as shavings, lightly taking on the warmth of a prepared dish. It would be wasteful to use it in a cooked dish.

I have included this truffle because I could not bear to leave it out.

Unlike the truffles above, the Italian White truffle
has a relatively smooth peridium and is more of a
yellowy to pale brown colour.

In Days Gone By

On a slightly lighter note, truffle sales today are probably a little more reliable than they used to be. Just for fun, let's look at what used to happen.

When the equivalent of truffle door-to-door salesmen used to exist, apparently a piece of coal might be put in amongst a bag of truffles so that there appeared to be more than there really were. Well, either housewives were easily fooled or the 'salesman' was operating out of his area... No-one would do that to me twice!

Then of course, was the problem of mud. Or should I describe it as an opportunity? It really depends on whether you are buying or selling. If you are selling by weight, a little extra mud might just help the family finances. Such a natural scenario, well, simply can't be helped.

Mud of course has other qualities too. It helps to coat the truffles to stop them drying out. Any good salesman would extol the virtues of mud.

And... mud is also extremely difficult to see through. It can hide a few small (but very heavy) pieces of lead shot pushed into the truffle.

And... mud can conveniently be packed into crevices or holes in the truffle to make it appear in good order.

And... mud can hide the joins where many small truffles are held together with sticks to make them appear as one.

And... mud can even disguise different kinds of truffles being passed off together.

Selling apples just doesn't offer the same scope.

At this Point in Time...

At the end of February 2010 we finally moved house. Both Paul and I tell everyone it was the outside of the house that made us buy it, not the inside. Of course we didn't want to plant a truffle orchard inside the house.

The acreage is slightly smaller than we were looking for, but with hindsight it is probably just as well the place was not bigger. I have some really useful space for the Dog School and some small little parcels of land divided up beautifully for dog training 'classrooms'.

Of course I have planted these up with authentic broadleaf woodland trees – all of which just happen to be truffle impregnated – remember those hazelnut bushes I bought at the end of 2006? Well, those went in and were followed by quite a few more too. At this time of writing, they have not yet produced any truffles but it is conceivable that we could be getting close. Just think, won't my customers have the luckiest dogs in the world when they can unearth a real truffle during lesson time – that has to be better than double maths any day!

The truffle orchard took a little more preparation. A couple of pig sties and an unwanted fence line went the journey, whilst new fencing was put in to confound the local rabbit and deer population. Paul does reminisce about his army days quite regularly and he would really love to have a turret-mounted machine gun for the squirrels. As yet, I've managed to persuade him against this, but if we ever suffer truffle poachers I'm sure he will raise the topic again.

The dormant tree season of 2010–11 saw Paul and I planting six hundred and fifty truffle impregnated trees. I have tried my hardest to remove the memories from my mind because the weather that winter was atrociously, diabolically horrible. Cold fingers, wet knees and sore backs were the norm as we tried to get a rhythm going. Measure the distance, deal out the posts, bang in the posts, dig out the hole, pop in the tree and slide over the guard. Phew! Now can you answer the question, "How long is a piece of string?" Well, we had the longest piece we could find as we triangulated all the distances to make sure our tree lines came out straight. Neither Paul nor I could bear wiggly lines. At least our efforts worked and now our orchard looks really, really smart.

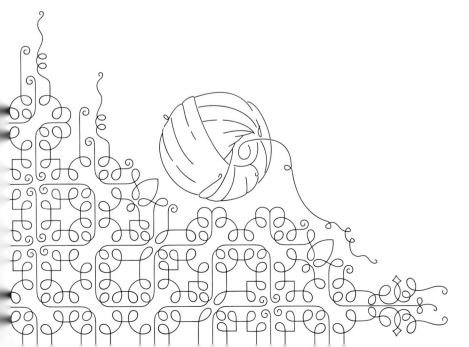

I'm pleased our orchard looks so smart. We watch it and wait.
We care for it and wait. We mow and mulch, weed and clear,
sample and test, and wait. Next, we have to wait some more.
It could be anything from five to ten years for the truffles to
start fruiting.

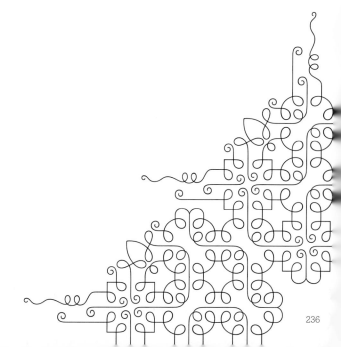

Truffles in Britain?

Yes, there most certainly are. Surely no-one can doubt it now?

There are some things in this world that are, well, just plain boring, and other things that are worth getting excited about. Truffles are worth it.

What we have done is to give you knowledge and opportunity. Seize them with both hands and make your own truffle journey. There is a wonderful road ahead of you.

Go forth: Experiment, Dare and Enjoy.

With thanks for your company and best wishes for the future,

Marions Dean and Pennington.

Printed in Great Britain by Berforts

www.berforts.co.uk
Telephone: +44 (0)1438 312777

Berforts Information Press Ltd
23-25 Gunnels Wood Park, Gunnels Wood Road
Stevenage, Hertfordshire SG1 2BH
United Kingdom